BOWLING STRIKES

DAWSON TAYLOR

**CONTEMPORARY
BOOKS**

CHICAGO

Library of Congress Cataloging-in-Publication Data

Taylor, Dawson.
    Bowling strikes / Dawson Taylor ; [introduction by Dave
Davis].
        p.   cm.
    Includes bibliographical references (p.   ) and index.
    ISBN 0-8092-3977-9
    1. Bowling.   I. Title.
GV903.T3   1991
794.6—dc20   91-24981
                                                          CIP

To Denny, Christine, and Dawson, and to
their most patient and understanding mother,
Mary Ellen, for their constant support and
encouragement

—Dawson Taylor

Interior photographs by Joaquin Bengochea
Copyright © 1991 by Dawson Taylor
All rights reserved
Published by Contemporary Books, Inc.
180 North Michigan Avenue, Chicago, Illinois 60601
Manufactured in the United States of America
International Standard Book Number: 0-8092-3977-9

Contents

Foreword

In 1976 I was bowling in a Professional Bowlers Association tournament in Miami, Florida, when Dawson Taylor introduced himself to me. He told me that in his opinion I was the "world's greatest bowler" and that, therefore, I should write a book which would make my knowledge of bowling and the secrets of my bowling technique accessible to every bowler.

I was aware that Dawson had written an earlier and highly successful book on bowling, *The Secret of Bowling Strikes*. Considering the matter carefully, I came to the conclusion that perhaps I could explain some of the reasons for my success in the lanes and thus help all bowlers enjoy the game more fully.

The result of Dawson's visit was that subsequently we collaborated on the writing of not one but two bowling books, *Winning Bowling* and *Earl Anthony's Championship Bowling*, both of which were published by Contemporary. Books, Inc. Those books have enjoyed excellent sales, with more than two hundred thousand copies now in the hands of bowlers all around the world.

Dawson Taylor has now been asked to write another bowling book to bring bowling instruction up-to-date and explain the changes in bowling equipment, lane conditioning, and modern strike bowling technique, most notably the "power ball," which has aided the phenomenal rise of Amleto Monacelli, a young Venezuelan who uses this technique with tremendous effect and success. I know that Dawson Taylor is an avid, discerning student of the sport of bowling. As a member of the Detroit Athletic Club and Detroit Golf Club leagues he was a many-time champion and averaged nearly 200 pins for more than 10 years. He knows what he is talking about when it comes to bowling and is especially expert on the mental side of bowling.

Without reservation, I highly recommend this new book by Dawson Taylor, *Bowling Strikes*. It may make you a champion, too!

—Earl Anthony
Cornelius, Oregon

Foreword

Earl Anthony and I both started on the Professional Bowlers Tour at nearly the same time, 35 years ago. I remember well some of our early head-to-head matches. As the years went on we met many times in preliminary rounds and in the finals of televised events. Sometimes I beat Earl, but more often I lost.

I was always envious of Earl's wonderful composure. A string of eight strikes in a row or a couple of wide-open splits brought the same wry smile to his face. He was simply the best in self-control, in my opinion, and as time went on his technique improved to the point that he won 32 championships and several million dollars in prize money along the way.

Earl Anthony and Dawson Taylor have teamed up to write two very successful bowling books. It is time now for another one which will make up-to-date knowledge about modern bowling technique and modern lane conditions readily available to scores of bowlers. I highly recommend this book to every bowler who wants to improve his game.

—Dave Davis

Preface

After World War II ended I returned to Detroit, Michigan, and entered the automobile business with my father and two brothers. Our dealership sponsored a bowling team in what was called the Classic League, one in which bowlers have no "spot" or handicap but bowl at scratch. This league had the best bowlers in the Midwest, and I had the privilege of watching such great bowlers as Don Carter, Billy Welu, Fred Bujack, Therman Gibson, Dick Weber, Basil "Buzz" Fazio, and many others as well.

It happened that we sold a new Dodge to Pete Carter, captain of the world champion Stroh's Beer bowling team. I talked to Pete about bowling and asked him to look me over with a view to improving my bowling score, which was then in the low 160s.

Pete and I went to a nearby bowling lane. I told him, "They say I have a good approach to the line, but when my ball hits the pins nothing happens. I get very few strikes and lots of splits."

Pete said, "Let me show you something," and with that he

put his bowling ball down on the approach and inserted just his third and fourth fingers. Suddenly he closed those fingers inside the ball as if he were snapping his fingers. The ball instantly started to revolve in a counterclockwise fashion.

I was amazed at the spinning action he had imparted to the ball. I asked him to show me again what he had done. Once more he put his third and fourth fingers into the ball, but this time he put his thumb in as well. Again, he snapped those fingers shut and the ball spun counterclockwise.

"See," he said, "how the thumb comes out first and then how the fingers put the spin on the ball. If you don't do it that way, the ball merely rolls end over end without any action on it. When it strikes the pins it deflects away from the 5 pin, which is the kingpin, and must be hit in order to cause all 10 pins to go down."

A light began to dawn in my mind. At last I could see why I had no power on my bowling ball. I did not have that finger action Pete was showing me. I thanked Pete very much and went home resolved to perfect that finger action myself.

I would put my bowling ball down on the floor of my vinyl-tiled recreation room and practice closing my fingers in the strike action Pete had shown me. I even went so far as to practice tossing the spinning ball into an old leather chair seat. It was a heavy piece of furniture and could withstand the shock of the 16-pound bowling ball. I would start three or four feet away and toss the ball, lifting it, squeezing my fingers in their fingerholes as I delivered the ball into the chair seat.

Very soon I began to notice an improvement in bowling my strike ball. At last I had power at the pocket and began stringing strikes together. It took me several years of regular practice, not only in my basement recreation room, but also on nearby neighborhood lanes. At last I saw wonderful results. My strike average climbed to four or even five strikes a game.

As a result of my improved strike ability, in the next 10 years I won no less than 20 bowling championships at the Detroit Athletic Club and the Detroit Golf Club, averaging from 190 to 199 pins per season. One season I needed 627 pins on my last bowling night to attain a 200 average. I failed by a few pins and had to settle for a 199 average.

Remember that I was a businessman bowler, bowling twice a week in club leagues. I'll admit that I sneaked out frequently at noon to practice, but I was not and am not a professional bowler.

Soon after I had achieved the ability to roll a strong strike ball I found myself teaching other bowlers who were rolling weak balls. Other bowlers caught onto the secret quickly, and not long afterward I wrote a book, *The Secret of Bowling Strikes*, which was published by A. S. Barnes and Co.

In the following years I have written three more books, *Mastering Bowling*, then *Winning Bowling*, and *Earl Anthony's Championship Bowling*, with famous bowling champion Earl Anthony, who so kindly has contributed a foreword for this book. Earl is the greatest bowling champion of them all, possessor of 32 Professional Bowlers Association Tour victories and winner of more than $2,000,000 in prize money. I appreciate his friendship very much, and his counsel on the writing of this book has been invaluable.

I have followed the progress of the wonderful sport of bowling for many years. I have seen the innovations in bowling balls, pins, lanes, and other new equipment, all of which have resulted in higher scores for the average bowler.

The game has changed in the last 20 years. We have seen the advent of the plastic pin, the plastic bowling ball, and plastic surfaces on the lanes. Scores have risen dramatically. The leading bowler in my old league now carries a 215 average.

It is time to review the secret of bowling the strike ball and tie it in with the innovations in pins, balls, and lane surfaces. This book is a complete textbook for every bowler from beginner to high average. If you will study and practice the method of "the squeeze," your bowling average will inevitably climb.

I wish you every success not only in raising your bowling average but also in understanding the physics and mental side of bowling.

I wish you good bowling!

Acknowledgments

I would like to thank the following people very much for their help on this book: first of all, Earl Anthony for his inspiration and for his kindness in contributing the foreword; Dave Davis for his counsel; Trudy Talia for her encouragement; models Judi and Christopher Wojcik and Robert and Margaret Bolds; and Joaquin Bengochea, a great sports photographer.

_____ PART I

THE FIRST BALL
_____

Understanding the Principle of the Squeeze

Before you read this book I would like you to perform several physical acts that will help you understand the principle of "the squeeze," the finger action necessary to produce strike power at the 1-3 pocket of the pin setup.

Put your bowling ball on the floor in front of you. With your thumbhole to the left, insert your third and fourth fingers into the ball. *Do not insert your thumb.* Pretend you are snapping your fingers inside the ball. You will find that the ball will at once start to rotate to the left. The force with which your fingers snapped is commensurate with the amount of power you imparted to the ball. Now try the same exercise, but this time with your thumb inserted into the thumbhole. Once again the ball will rotate to the left, but that thumb must get out of its hole before the fingers can do their work.

For the second exercise, have a friend stand in front of you as you hold your bowling ball in your hand. Open your wrist to the right so that your thumb and your third and fourth fingers are all pointing at your friend. Have him pull the ball away from you slowly. Note that all the fingers leave the ball

1

at the same time. There is no question of any ability of the fingers to remain in the ball and give it any "snapping" or "squeeze" action.

Put your hand into the bowling ball as you normally would, thumb at the 11 o'clock or 10 o'clock position, fingers in their finger holes. Have your friend pull the ball away from you as he did before. This time you will clearly see that because the thumb leaves the ball well before the fingers do, the fingers now can act in the squeeze fashion.

This is also a clear demonstration of the necessity for the bowler to deliver the ball out over the foul line so that the thumb can leave the ball first and let the third and fourth fingers do the work of "squeezing," imparting spin, "action," "finger-lift," "turn," "power," "snap," or "stuff" on the ball, all of which terms are used and have been used for years by bowlers to describe the powerful strike ball.

THE SQUEEZE

There are many secrets to becoming a good bowler, but there is one in particular that every bowler must know in order to be a champion. It is the secret of putting action into the bowling ball, that is, imparting the spin that causes the ball to hook strongly into the 1-3 strike pocket and gives it enough power to carry through to the 5 pin and cause all 10 pins to fall for a strike.

This secret is called by various names—lift, finger-lift, action—but the most descriptive name for it is *the squeeze.* The action of the fingers in lifting the ball at the delivery point (the foul line) is not unlike the finger action you would use to squeeze a small ball in the palm of your hand, clenching the third and fourth fingers against the palm of your hand. When this finger action is used while the ball is leaving your hand at the foul line, the result is a lift or squeeze on the ball. This squeeze causes the ball to begin to rotate on an axis to the left-hand side of the headpin (for right-handed bowlers). After its initial momentum has carried it about 20 feet down the lane, the ball begins to roll on that axis and hook in toward the pocket.

The accompanying photographs give you a graphic idea of the squeeze and show how you can practice the finger action in the privacy of your own home until you can accomplish it on every delivery. Once you have learned the secret of the squeeze, you are on your way to becoming a good bowler.

Is there a secret to throwing a strike ball every time you roll it down the lane? Yes, there is and it's called *the squeeze*.

This ball has been lofted out over the foul line and in mid-air is continuing to rotate to the left on a 4 o'clock to 10 o'clock axis. The bowler's fingers have yet to close completely in the squeeze.

Here's how to understand the principle of the squeeze. Put your ball down on the lane in front of you and insert only your third and fourth fingers. Close them quickly and observe how the ball starts to spin counterclockwise.

The Four Fundamentals of Bowling

Here are the four absolute fundamentals of an effective, repeating bowling delivery. All must be present in order to carry strikes with the first ball and convert spares and splits on the second ball.

1. A smooth, rhythmic, four-step (or more) approach to the foul line takes the bowler to the point of delivery in perfect balance at the exact time the bowling arm passes his left ankle.
2. The bowler's body must be square to the line of intended travel by the bowling ball.
3. There must be a consciously executed effort by the bowler to impart spin to the ball at the moment of delivery, that fraction of a second when the ball passes the bowler's left ankle as he slides to the line. This finger, hand, and wrist action is the squeeze and results in the ball's rotating counterclockwise as it slides and rolls down the lane eventually to hook into the 1-3 pocket.

4. The bowler must keep his eyes on a definite target spot or line, usually at the break of the boards, as he delivers the ball out onto the lane with from 12 to 14 inches of loft. He must *stay down* with the shot, following straight through with his right shoulder, hand, and arm until his ball is well down the lane.

The Deliveries

Four steps are the accepted and recommended number of steps to be learned in bowling. While there are other step patterns, the four-step approach is considered the simplest to learn. It is easier, more functional, and less apt to cause timing troubles for the bowler in synchronizing his swing and foot movement. Once the bowler has perfected the four-step delivery, he may later on with caution experiment with the other types of delivery.

Take a natural step forward on the right foot at the same instant that the ball is pushed away from the body. On the first step the left hand is still supporting the ball. The mere weight of the ball sends it forward and downward into the start of the bowling swing.

On the second step the ball is at the bowler's side and begins to move into the lower portion of the backswing as the left foot touches the floor in the approach to the line. The right arm is held close to the body, and the left arm instinctively starts to seek a natural balancing position without any help from the bowler.

The ball reaches the top of the backswing toward the end of the third step. Momentum is increasing, and the arm is still straight, swinging freely from the shoulder. The first two steps and the movement of the body supply the necessary acceleration. At the end of the third step the ball should be at the peak of the backswing—never higher than the shoulder—and the shoulder should be parallel to the foul line. The downward movement of the ball starts easily and the knees begin to bend, lowering the bowler's body to prepare for the final step on the left foot.

This last step is a long slide that generally ends an inch or two in front of the foul line. As long as you maintain consistency, this distance from the foul line may vary a few inches without problems. However, your lateral position should remain constant; that is, you should not be at the center of the lane one time and more to one side at another time.

On the fourth step the knee is bent and you slide on your left foot. Your heel strikes the surface of the lane as your knee straightens out. The rubber heel of your shoe acts as a brake to stop you at the line. The ball and the left foot should reach the foul line at the same time. The body bends forward in delivering the ball over the foul line. There is a distinct follow-through with the right arm and shoulder as the ball leaves your hand. The ball can be delivered naturally, without any attempt on your part to twist your wrist at the moment of delivery, or you may aid the delivery with what is called a lift or turn. The fingers of your hand close as the ball leaves the hand, with the thumb coming out of its hole first. With a squeezing, finger-snapping, lifting motion of the two fingers that have remained in the ball, the ball is given a rotating momentum which it carries a distance down the lane until its skidding momentum ends and the hooking action begins.

There is no essential difference between the four-step delivery and a five-step delivery. Basically, the five-step delivery is a four-step delivery with the ball carried on the first step. The timing is the same once the four-step ball-pushaway action begins. Some bowlers prefer the five-step delivery because it feels more natural for them to start on the left foot. The five-step delivery also helps if your strides are too long. Necessarily you must shorten your steps or go over the foul line. The bowler who prefers a faster approach finds the five-step delivery more suitable.

In the four-step delivery your weight starts out on the left foot; it is transferred to your right foot as you step forward with the right. In the five-step delivery, the reverse is true, of course, with the weight starting out on the right side and then transferring to the left as the left foot takes the first of the five steps. You should have the feeling that your body is moderately erect throughout your approach to the foul line. Actually, it starts to lean forward midway in the delivery as the ball forces the body downward when the arm goes backward for the backswing.

At the same time that you shift your weight forward onto the foot that is taking the first of the last four steps to the line, push the ball away from your body until your arms are fully extended in front of you. You do not want to lift the ball upward from its original position in your stance, nor do you want to drop it prematurely into its downswing. As both arms reach the fully extended position, the left hand smoothly lets the right hand take care of the problem of what to do with the ball. It is as if the left hand is offering the ball to the right hand, saying, "All right, now it's your turn."

When you push the ball straight out from your starting position at waist level, the ball will be in front of you, ready to swing from a height sufficient to give it a good momentum. This start of your pushaway should be as free and unrestricted as possible. Try not to muscle the ball or limit its swing in any way. In other words, let the ball do the work it is intended to do. You are going to act as the intermediary that lets it proceed through its backswing, stop at the top of the backswing, and proceed through the downswing and explosion point at the line.

I merely suggest that you should try starting your delivery with the ball at waist level first. Many excellent bowlers use this waist-high pushaway, and one cannot argue with their success. But we will also examine some alternatives: for example, the chest-high dropaway or the tentative low-swing start used by Marshall Holman and others.

Once your right heel has accepted your body weight and started you on your straight-ahead footwork toward the line and your ball reaches its fully extended position at the end of your outstretched right hand, you are committed to that swing. Any error you make at this point will affect the ball swing. That is why it is so important for you to develop and perfect a consistent pushaway in which your arm not only extends the same distance in front of your body every time but also creates the same angle with the front of your body.

It is obvious that if you push the ball out to belt height on one delivery, to an inch below belt height on the next, and then to an inch above belt height on a third successive delivery, you are adding a variation to your bowling swing that will lead to inconsistent timing at the foul line. It is essential that you have the physical ability to do something with the ball just when it reaches the bottom of its arc at the foul line; any inconsistency hinders this ability.

Try not to vary the way you start the ball in motion on your first step. If you habitually hold it in front of you at belt height, check yourself on every delivery to see that you are holding it at this height—no higher and no lower—and that your arm is extended precisely the same distance from your body every time.

If, as you bowl, you discover that you need more or less speed on the ball, then and only then should you change the way you start the ball in motion. Of course, you can and should experiment in practice by trying the ball an inch or so higher or lower at the start, with your arm more or less extended from your body, but once you have chosen an exact method, try not to vary it.

The squeeze, or lift, of the bowling ball may be accompanied by what is called turn or wrist turn. Basically, there are two styles of bowling delivery: those with no wrist turn at the explosion point and those with wrist turn at the explosion point.

The bowler who releases the ball with no wrist turn merely keeps the wrist in the same position throughout the backswing and forward swing, with the thumb on the inside of the ball (toward the body). With no effort to rotate the wrist in a counterclockwise fashion, he or she merely lets the ball come off the hand naturally, releasing the thumb first because it is shorter than the rest of the fingers. At the last second of the release, the bowler imparts the squeeze or lift to the ball as it finally leaves the fingers.

The bowler who employs wrist turn releases the ball after a distinct turn of the wrist from, say, a 6 o'clock to 3 o'clock finger position. The thumb moves inside the ball from 12 o'clock to 10 o'clock (on the way to 9 o'clock but never quite reaching it), at which point the thumb pulls out of the ball and allows the fingers to impart the squeeze or lift from a 3 o'clock to a 9 o'clock position. If the thumb passes 9 o'clock on its way from 12 o'clock, the ball has been turned too much and will have poor action.

The bowler who uses wrist turn on the delivery must be careful to use it in the same way every time. That means that you will not be consistent if you release the ball with a turn from 6 o'clock to 4 o'clock one time and from 6 o'clock to 3 o'clock another time.

Each bowler must decide which delivery method to use according to which feels most natural. Once you decide on the wrist-turn method, you must concentrate on consistently using the same hand, wrist, and finger action every time.

The photos on the following pages illustrate some tips to help you develop a strong delivery.

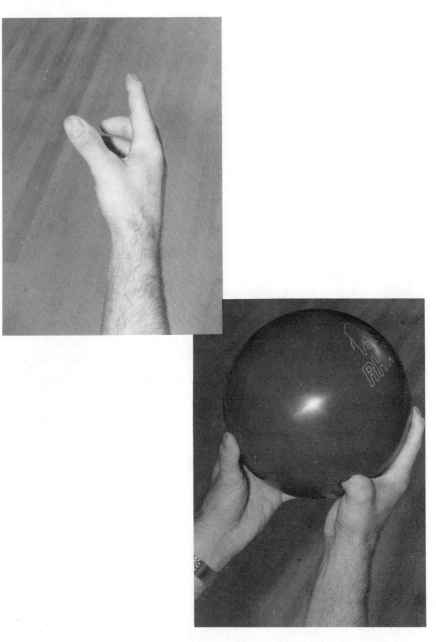

The photo on the left illustrates what the bowler should imagine as he holds his ball. He should visualize his fingers inside the ball with his thumb pointing to the o'clock position he wants at the delivery, whether 10 o'clock or 11 o'clock or even 9 o'clock if he wants the very powerful delivery from that position.

In that fraction of a
second as the bowler's
thumb exits the ball, his
fingers are ready to
impart the squeeze.

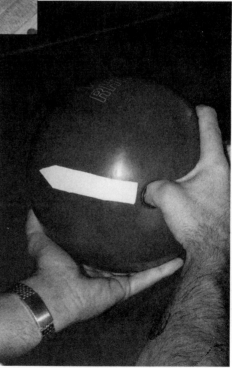

The bowler's hand is ready
to deliver a ball on a 3
o'clock to 9 o'clock axis, a
very powerful ball. Note
how the left hand
supports the ball until it is
ready to drop away into
the backswing.

The bowler prepares to deliver the ball on a 4 o'clock to 10 o'clock axis. This hand position results in a strong ball that will deliver a lot of power at the 1-3 pocket and is the most common hand position among bowlers.

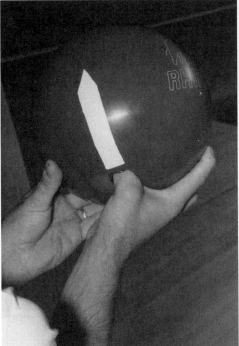

The bowler's hand position is ready to deliver the ball on a 5 o'clock to 11 o'clock axis. Although this style of delivery does not result in as powerful a ball as the 10 o'clock or 9 o'clock positions do, it is more accurate, delivering plenty of power at the pocket.

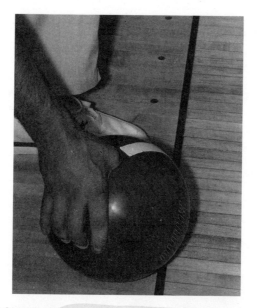

The ball rolls from 4 o'clock to 10 o'clock and results in a strong hook at the end of travel down the lane. This is the most popular style of delivery and is adaptable to nearly all lane conditions.

For a 5 o'clock to 11 o'clock roll on the ball, the hand is kept well behind the ball and the thumb points toward 11 o'clock on an imaginary clock dial. The hook on this ball is only moderate, but it is very accurate.

The straight ball rolls practically end over end and has little if any turn at the end of its roll. The hand is kept directly behind the ball, and no squeeze is applied at the last moment.

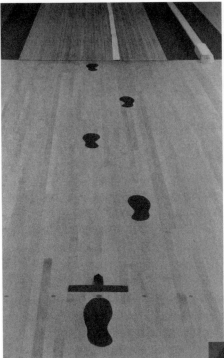

The four-step delivery is the most common in bowling. It is rhythmic and the pace of the downswing, backswing, and forward swing of the ball coincide very well with the bowler's steps as he approaches the foul line. The ball passes his left ankle at the same moment his hand, wrist, and arm are ready to deliver the ball out over the foul line with the squeeze.

The first step of the three-step delivery is taken with the left foot. This delivery requires considerable strength of body and arm and is compact and effective, but sometimes it is difficult to develop enough ball speed with the three-step delivery.

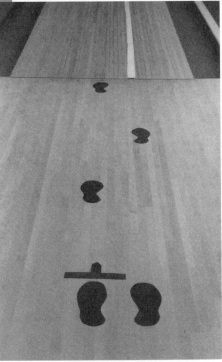

In the most common starting position the ball is held comfortably in the extended right arm and right hand. The left hand helps support the ball until he is ready to drop it away into its downward arc at the exact instant he moves his right foot forward in his first step.

In this variation of the starting position the bowler holds the ball up high, close to his body, and pushes it out with a motion which coincides with the first step of a four-step delivery. In the five-step delivery he will carry the ball for the first step and then drop it away. This is a powerful style: the arc of the ball is longer than usual, and thus the bowler generates more speed. However, it is harder to control than the more conventional delivery with the ball held lower at the start.

Another common variation in the starting position has been made popular by such bowling stars as Marshall Holman and Wayne Webb. The bowler crouches over, holding the ball very low. He dangles it back and forth until he senses the proper moment to start his delivery.

The bowler must have the feeling that he is "square" to his intended line through his hips, his body, and his followthrough straight down the lane. The foul line is parallel to a line through the bowler's hips at the delivery point.

The Cupped-Wrist Power Ball

About 10 years ago the sport of bowling saw the introduction of a radically different style of delivery known as *the power ball.*

Instead of maintaining a firm, unbent wrist in his backswing, the power bowler cups the ball in his hand and arm, letting the ball rest on his forearm during an extra long backswing. This hand and wrist position sounds awkward, and it is, but the strange truth of the matter is that when the power bowler brings his arm, hand, and wrist back to the delivery point he achieves what amounts to a slingshot effect. It is as if the ball has been given a running start at the pins.

The effect of such a ball is simply unbelievable at times. The wrist becomes firm at the delivery point and the squeeze is imparted to the ball as it is projected out onto the lane. The cupped wrist, in returning to what might be called the normal firm wrist position, adds considerable speed and power to the final snap of the fingers and wrist as the ball leaves the fingers. The ball is whipped down the lane, slung like a rock from a slingshot.

In the extreme 3 o'clock to 9 o'clock roll of the cupped-wrist power ball, the hand remains on the side of the ball. The lift or wrist turn is straight across toward 3 o'clock on the imaginary clock dial. It is an extremely powerful ball but difficult for the average bowler to roll because it requires a great deal of physical strength.

The power ball must necessarily be delivered from an inside angle far to the right side of the lane. The ball comes dangerously close to going into the channel before it assumes its eventual move back to the left into the pocket. It can be rolled into an area down the lane rather than straight down a particular line and into the pocket. When the power ball hits the pocket it comes in at about a 75- to 80-degree angle (not far from a 90-degree angle, but that would be impossible to do). The ball creates such side-to-side reaction that the bowler can almost count on pin action causing the pins to fly off the sideboards and plough across the pin setup, taking out any stubborn pins left standing.

Notice that the bowler's hand is turned backward in what is called the cupped-wrist position. The bowler continues to keep this wrist position as well as he can throughout his armswing until the moment of truth at delivery over the line when the wrist returns to firmness and allows the fingers to squeeze the ball and loft it out over the foul line.

At the top of the backswing of the cupped-wrist power ball delivery, the wrist is still somewhat cupped, but not as much as it was at the start. This allows for some of the whipping action at the delivery point. It is almost a slingshot effect and results in a very powerful ball, but it's very difficult to control and requires a great deal of practice.

There is just one thing for the average bowler to note, however. The power ball is rolled by professional bowlers who roll from 25 to 100 games a day in practice. It is extremely difficult to control, even by the professional. The slingshot effect does not always work or, if it does, it works in an erratic fashion, giving 80 percent power one time, 90 percent the next, and then 50 percent.

When the power ball fails to hit the pocket the bowler is often faced with a split or an awkward and difficult spare. Several times in recent months top professional bowlers such as Marshall Holman and Don Ballard have rolled gutter balls in crucial strike situations. Holman, incredibly, rolled two gutter balls in succession in a final game on television's Professional Bowlers Association Tour. It is most probable that both bowlers were attempting to roll power balls and simply failed to give their bowling balls the usual power lift at the line.

Can you, the average bowler, use the power ball style of delivery? Perhaps. You might experiment with it. It takes a great deal of physical strength in the fingers, wrist, and arm—indeed, in the entire body—to make the delivery successful. If you cannot control it, I recommend that you go back to the traditional style of delivery and perfect that. You may not get as many power strikes, but you will not get as many misses or splits, either.

Balance

It is obvious to most bowlers, especially early in their careers, that that 16-pound ball sometimes acts in a devilish fashion that will throw a bowler off balance. The more you observe the good bowlers you see that none of them allows the ball to get very far away from the body. Some bowlers even exaggerate how close they carry the ball to the right side of the body while remaining very upright in vertical fashion all through the approach and delivery. An upright posture does tend to keep the arm and ball close to the side of the body. If it can be achieved along with a full, smooth delivery, it might be your answer to the problem of imbalance.

On the other hand, if it feels unnatural to you to be extremely erect, then allow the ball and your arm to find a groove slightly away from your body but as close to it as your musculature and body movements will allow. Definitely do not allow the right arm to get away from the body any more than you have to; otherwise, you will find yourself suffering a loss of balance at the delivery and the ball may end up careening from right to left across your body, missing the headpin to the left.

Do not bend to the left, to the right, or too far forward. As the ball goes into its backswing, your upper body naturally tilts forward and accepts the tension of the right arm muscles on the backswing. In fact, this forward lean must take place, or else the backswing will be cramped and unnatural.

There is an old adage in bowling that your nose should never pass in front of your knees. This is a good rule to observe. You do not want to bend forward during your slide and release.

Slide by bending your left knee and keeping it bent, and remember to try to keep your upper body erect. This erect, square-to-the-line approach allows your entire body to stay with the ball and to follow it with your arm a little longer. In addition, it often allows you to impart a little more snap to the release than usual, giving the ball extra power that shows up at the pocket in more action.

Grips

There are three common varieties of bowling grips: conventional, fingertip, and semi-fingertip. The first, conventional, is one in which your third and fourth fingers are inserted into the ball up to the second knuckle joints. The fingertip grip is just what it sounds like, a grip in which the bowler uses only the fingertips of the third and fourth fingers in the ball. The semi-fingertip grip is in between the other two grips in that the pads of flesh between the first and second joints are used.

The conventional grip is recommended for beginning bowlers and those bowlers who carry about a 150 to 165 average. The conventionally drilled ball is the easiest to control. Until the bowler reaches maximum control over the ball, he should remain with the conventional grip. Then, and only then, should he begin to experiment with either the semi-fingertip or the full fingertip drillings.

These latter grips require considerably more finger, hand, and wrist strength than the conventional grip. The bowler must work on increasing his strength so that he can not only

In the proper grip the fingers are firm but not tense. If anything, they are on the relaxed side. The hand is on the side of the ball with the thumb inside it pointing to an imaginary 10 o'clock on a clock dial. It may point to 11 o'clock for some bowlers, but in general will never point any farther to the left than 9 o'clock. The ball is supported by the left hand and arm as the left hand and arm prepare to drop the ball away into its downswing.

hold the ball securely throughout his swing, but also control it at the explosion point of delivery.

Champion bowler Earl Anthony demonstrates the fingertip grip he has used to win 32 Professional Bowlers Association championships. Such a grip requires much wrist, finger, and hand strength, but the power that results is well worth the effort.

The fingers stay in the ball longer in the semi-fingertip and fingertip grips than they do in the conventional grip. At first, your accuracy will suffer as you learn to control the ball from the new position. You will find that you have more power or action on the ball because your thumb leaves the ball sooner than it did with the conventional grip, thus increasing the time the ball is held only by your fingers.

It may take you months of finger, hand, and wrist strengthening exercises to feel confident that you can hold the ball with only your fingertips. Once you have that control and have also been able to deliver the ball with as much accuracy as you had before switching your drilling, you will never go back to the conventional grip again. (Examples of finger, hand, and wrist strengthening exercises are given in Tip 5.)

The Bowling Ball

BALL FIT

It is most important that you acquire and use a bowling ball that literally fits like a glove. This is not an easy task, and you may find that you will have to try many different balls before you finally have the one that suits your hand and works well for you.

Primarily, you want a ball that does not cause any undue wear on your fingers, particularly your thumb. If your thumb does not come out of the ball smoothly and catches or rubs either side of the thumbhole, you may end up with a blister at the base of your thumb or on one side of it, and your bowling will be affected adversely. You may have to bandage it with collodion and cotton batting and continue to bowl with an awkward inconsistent grip.

You must trust your local ball driller in this matter. He will work with you like a doctor of medicine to find your ideal ball-drilling specifications. From then on in your bowling career you can use the same finger spans and pitches to acquire other carbon-copy balls with different balances and surfaces that affect the final snap of the ball into the 1-3 pocket.

Interestingly, Hall of Fame Bowler Dave Davis told me that a few years ago Amleto Monacelli came all the way up to New Jersey from Venezuela to have Davis drill several bowling balls for him. The drillings must have been good for, as we know, Monacelli went on to become the 1990 Bowler of the Year on the Professional Bowlers Association Tour.

You must have confidence in your ball driller. In every city there is at least one who is known to other bowlers, especially the good bowlers, as the expert in that area. You should seek him out. It will be well worth your effort and will pay off in a higher average and less wear on your fingers.

Ball-fitting is a difficult problem that can be solved only by an expert. There are no less than 12 individual measurements that must be taken into consideration in drilling and preparing a properly fitted bowling ball. Some of them are so technical that we will not discuss them here. You will have to rely on the expert judgment of your ball driller for more detailed explanations.

Let us say that you have found the best ball driller in your area and have arranged to have him drill your new bowling ball. He will use an interesting ball-fitting device, which has many finger holes, sizes, and pitches. Your thumbhole will be measured first because it is the most important of the three finger holes to be drilled.

If the thumbhole is drilled and fitted improperly for you, your thumb will release either too soon or too late. If it releases too soon, you will have one or more of the following problems at the delivery point of the bowling swing:

1. You will drop the ball short of the foul line.
2. You will be unable to apply the proper lift with your fingers.
3. You will come up short on your slide to the line.
4. You will drop your shoulder at the line.
5. You will be forced to squeeze the ball in order to hang onto it and thus will deliver it in inconsistent fashion, hanging onto it one time and not hanging onto it the next.

If your thumb comes out too late in the delivery, there is less time between that instant of thumb exit and the time when your fingers execute the squeeze. To compensate, you might find yourself concentrating on what your thumb is doing, not on your target and target line. The result is disturbed aim and inconsistency.

An excellent rule to follow at the start is to have your thumbhole drilled $\frac{3}{64}$ of an inch larger than the smallest hole your thumb will enter without forcing it in or out of the hole. There should be no drag, just easy entrance and exit. Ask the ball driller not to make the hole too large at the start of the ball-drilling process. Let him know that you want to begin with a snug thumbhole and gradually enlarge it to allow the exact ease of exit you want. It may be necessary for you to return to the driller several times to obtain this kind of fit.

To determine whether or not your ball fits your hand, first check the thumb fit. Put your thumb all the way into the thumbhole. If there is any room for sideways movement, the hole is too big for you. If your thumb is pinched or pulled as you snap your thumb out of the hole, the hole is too small for you. You should be able to feel the surface of the thumbhole all around your thumb when it is inserted fully into the hole.

Here is another good rule to follow in trying to determine whether or not you have a good thumb fit. If you cannot hold your bowling ball with just the thumb in the ball, the thumbhole is too large for you or the ball is too heavy. The weight of the ball is held primarily by the thumb until the moment of release, at which time the weight of the ball is transferred to the inside of the fingers.

The finger holes, however, should not fit too tightly. If the finger holes are too tight, a vacuum effect may be evidenced by a popping sound as the fingers come out; the result will be a drag on the ball rather than the free release you always seek. When the finger holes are too tight, the finger releases will be inconsistent, leading to inconsistent ball action.

It is very useful to have your finger holes drilled to the precise and exact depth of your fingertips. Drilling deeper than those positions leads to irregular placement of the fin-

It is a good idea to individualize your bowling balls by using distinctive markings or advice. One of my own bowling balls is marked my *B* ball, which meant that it was not too strong, not too weak. The letters *TYT* told me, "Take your time." The five *X*s reminded me to concentrate on getting strikes, five in a row if I could. Note, too, the drilling to the right of my fourth finger, a locator spot that helped me keep my little finger in the same position at delivery.

gers and inconsistent delivery. You will have to work with your ball driller on these exact drillings, but the result is well worth the effort of returning to have "just a little more" material taken out of a finger hole.

If you find that you are losing the ball before you want to release it or before you expect to, remember that the culprit will be your thumbhole, not the finger hole.

BALL WEIGHT

If your ball is too heavy, you may find that you have trouble controlling it. Your ability to aim will be decreased. You will miss your target more often and therefore will miss more spares and strike pockets than you would if you had better control. With a lighter ball you may be inclined to use too much control, aiming the ball instead of letting it roll freely. You will not have as much power at the pocket with a lighter ball and may lose some strikes as a result. It is obvious that you have to make a compromise somewhere between using a heavy ball and a lighter one. Knowing what may or may not happen when you use each kind will help you make up your mind. Life is a compromise at times—so is bowling!

The Horseshoe-Pitching Concept

Midway in my bowling career I was carrying an average in the high 180s to low 190s. At that time we moved our residence from the northwest side of Detroit to the community of Bloomfield Hills, outside the city.

My wife and I bought the house in a hurry one Sunday afternoon in spring. When the final closing of the transaction had been completed we became aware that not only had we bought the beautiful new house, but we now were also the possessors of an undeveloped acre of land behind it.

Once we moved in, my wife decided that we should have a flower and vegetable garden in the so-called back acre. We found that it took a great deal of physical effort to clear the land. The back acre was on top of a centuries-old alluvial deposit of gravel ranging from egg-sized rocks to rocks as large as an indoor baseball and sometimes even larger and heavier—as large as melons.

Night after night, I was the one who had to pick up those stones and toss them over the lot line into a nearby wooded area. I found myself hurling the rocks underhand in my usual bowling motion and took a lot of pleasure out of realizing that not only was I "de-rocking" the garden but I was also practicing my bowling ball release as I tossed the heavy rocks fifteen or twenty yards away.

Lo! and behold, that season my bowling average jumped up another four pins. For a while I carried an even 200 average. I am convinced that my outdoor rock-tossing was the cause of it.

It might be difficult for you to find a similar rock pile and start tossing the rocks as I did. However, along the same line of thought, I would like to call your attention to the concept of the horseshoe pitcher and his style of throwing horseshoes at the stake 40 feet away from him. The free motion of the horseshoe pitcher is exactly what the bowler wants to imitate in his delivery of the bowling ball straight down his target line to the bowling-pin setup.

Several famous bowlers of our day were and are great horseshoe pitchers. Eddie Lubanski of the champion Detroit Stroh's bowling team in the 1950s was a horseshoe pitching champion. He rolled a two-fingered ball with devastating effect. His delivery was smooth and full with a free-flowing followthrough.

Walter Ray Williams, Jr., became a professional bowler after years of success as a horseshoe pitching champion. Walter has won the World Series of horseshoe pitching no less than four times, most recently in 1989. His percentage of ringers, incidentally, is a phenomenal 92.29 percent, which means he throws a ringer nine times out of ten. Walter led the Professional Bowlers Association Tour for the 1986 Winter Tour with earnings of $131,835 and was named PBA Player of the Year. He has earned more than three-quarters of a million dollars in prize money in the last nine years of the PBA Tour. Walter agrees with me that bowling and horseshoes are very similar in technique. "It's all basically a matter of the armswing," he says.

Eddie Lubanski and many others, too, have become great bowlers after learning to throw horseshoes successfully. Whether you take up horseshoe pitching or "de-rocking" of

Walter Ray Williams, Jr.,
shows his championship
horseshoe-pitching form
that led him to become a
champion bowler as well.

gardens (as I did), I suggest that you keep in your mind's eye
the picture of the free-throwing horseshoe pitcher, his backswing, his downswing, his extremely long follow-through. See
how square to the line his body is. He is throwing down a
straight line to the stake. He has confidence that if he has the
proper distance he will score a ringer. Moreover, he is not
trying to force the horseshoe or bend it in flight. He is trusting
his swing to do the work.

When you bowl I would like you to picture yourself as a
horseshoe pitcher who just happens to have a bowling ball in
his hand. Let the ball do the work in your backswing and
forward swing. Let the ball come off your hand without any
undue effort to steer it or to control the direction at the last
second. Have confidence that your last-second squeeze will set
it spinning straight down the lane to your target.

If you can impress upon your mind that image of the free-
stroking, rhythmic horseshoe pitcher, I truly believe you will
become a better bowler.

The Archer/Bow and Arrow Concept

Another mental picture I would like you to visualize is that of the archer in motion. Picture yourself on an outdoor 100-yard range with a strong wind blowing directly from right to left.

You aim your first arrow at the bull's-eye and find that it strikes two feet to the left of the target. You correct your aim to take into consideration the way the wind has moved your arrow in flight and aim your next shot two feet to the right of the target. You let the arrow fly, and presto! You hit the bull's-eye.

In bowling you must have the same confidence that the archer has in calculating his windage to the target. You, too, will aim at an imaginary target to the right of your true target and will let the action or curve of your ball bring it over into the 1-3 pocket successfully.

The Dynamics of Bowling Ball Action

In order to be successful, you must send the bowling ball down the lane on a particular path. It must roll down the right-hand side of the lane to a crucial spot a few feet from the pins. It must then hook sharply to the left and clip the front pin, the 1 pin, and the pin just behind it, the 3 pin, in such a precise way that the front pin will knock down the three pins on the left-hand side of the triangle of pins. Meanwhile, the ball continues rolling with power into the remaining three pins—the center one, which is the so-called kingpin of the group, and the two behind it—to topple them, too. If a bowler sends a ball straight down the lane into the 1-3 pocket (or the 1-2 pocket for the left-hander) without a quick turn incorporated into the trajectory, the neat sequence of falling dominoes will take place infrequently.

No good bowlers, professional or amateur, roll a straight ball. They all throw a hook or at least use some semblance of curve on the ball.

The bowling ball normally skids after it first touches down on the lane beyond the foul line, then it hooks left, and finally it rolls straight ahead along the line that the hooking action has determined. The normal pattern of skid-hook-roll is 20 feet, 20 feet, and 20 feet, successively. When you find the ball going into its roll too soon and therefore hitting high on the headpin, you must adjust by placing the ball farther out on the lane. In that way you postpone the moment when the hook ends and the forward roll starts. The reverse is true, too, when the ball is not coming up to the pocket soon enough. You must start the ball closer to the foul line than usual, causing the hooking action to take place sooner and sending the ball into the pocket on time.

There is a happy medium you can aim for in the amount of speed needed for maximum action. An excessively slow ball is just as ineffective as a ball that is too fast. The slow ball causes the action to occur too soon; the fast ball, too late or not at all. Unless your ball is obviously too fast or too slow, try to work out a normal medium speed for yourself and

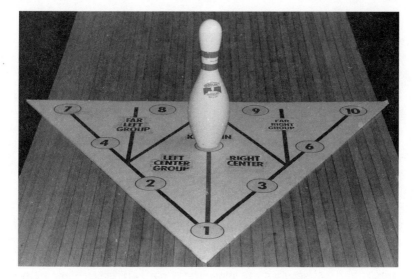

The 5 pin is called the kingpin for good reason. Without its help in transmitting the power of the ball to the other pins it is most difficult, if not impossible, to get a strike. It is your primary target in trying to get a strike. Always look for it before you bowl your first ball and concentrate on getting it out of the pin cluster.

adjust the hitting-the-pocket problem through changes and variation in your stance, your pushaway, your approach, and your target line.

UNDERSTANDING ANGLE

It is very important that the bowler understand the meaning and use of angle in knocking down the pins. The angle is the direction of the bowling ball as it enters the 1-3 pocket on the way to the 5 pin, which is the key, or kingpin, of the group. If you draw an imaginary line from the right-hand corner of a

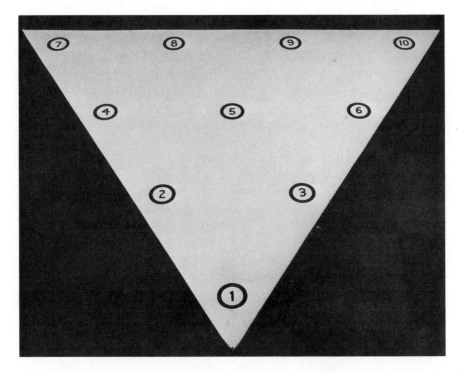

This is the full setup of 10 pins. The 5 pin is directly behind the headpin. It is the kingpin or key to carrying a strike on the first ball bowled. The pins are numbered in sequence starting with a 1 pin, the headpin. The 2 pin and the 3 pin are in the second row; the 4 pin, 5 pin, and 6 pin are in the third row; the 7 pin, 8 pin, 9 pin, and 10 pin are in the last row.

lane to the 5 pin, you will understand that the angle of entry of the line would be the correct angle to carry a strike.

When bowlers discuss angle, they refer only to the last few feet of travel by the ball before it crashes into the pocket. Therefore, it follows that if your bowling ball has a large hook at the end of its travel, it is necessary for you to deliver the ball at the start of its trip down the lane at a point somewhere near the center of the lane so that it can roll out to the right, then start to hook, and finally enter the pocket at the angle you need in order to carry a strike.

It is necessary to understand how the ball track affects angle, too. The bowling ball is 27 inches in circumference and about 9 inches wide at its equator. At its center, a bowling pin measures 4.7666 inches wide. If you add the width of the bowling pin to the width of the ball, doubled (remember, it can knock down the pin from either side), it is evident that the bowling track is nearly 23 inches.

Judi reminds us that we must keep our entire attention on the king-pin, the 5 pin, the key to getting pin action, which tumbles all the other pins.

The bowling ball is also subject to deflection as it strikes the pins. Go back into the pins some time and watch what happens when the ball strikes the pins. It bounces one way and another as its 16-pound weight is affected by the 3½-pound weight of the pins. The ball must strike a pin precisely head-on to avoid being deflected by it. Hit a pin on its side and the ball will move toward that side. That is one of the reasons why tandem spares are so difficult to convert. (Tandem spares are those in which one pin stands directly behind the other.)

You must learn to watch the angle your ball takes in entering the strike pocket. You will learn that if you frequently leave the 5 pin you need a greater angle to bring the ball farther in from the side to get to the 5 pin. Good bowlers are always aware of their bowling angle. You must be, too.

The third arrow line on the lane is one of the most common strike lines used by bowlers. One board to the left of that line is the Brooklyn or crossover line, which takes the ball into the 1-2 pocket.

BALL BALANCE

Under the rules of the American Bowling Congress (ABC), the size, weight, and construction of bowling balls are carefully controlled and specified. A bowling ball may not have a circumference of more than 27 inches or a weight of more than 16 pounds. The rules also provide that bowling balls shall be constructed so that no fewer than six sides be in proper balance.

Here is the interesting feature of that rule: "proper balance." Apparently the ABC rule makers realized that no bowling ball could be in perfect balance and allowed some tolerance for imbalance. The rules go on to say,

> The following tolerances shall be permissible in the balance of a bowling ball:
>
> 10 pounds or more—
> a. Not more than 3 ounces difference between top of ball (finger hole side) and the bottom (solid side opposite finger holes)
> b. Not more than 1 ounce difference between the sides to the right and left of the finger holes or between the sides in front and back of the finger holes.

Note: The rules go on to provide for weights and balances of balls that are less than 10 pounds, but since most bowlers will never use the light ball, we will not discuss those rules here.

As time went on and bowlers used balls with differing imbalances, it became clear that some effects of imbalance caused more action at the strike pocket than others. When the balance was improper, the ball sometimes actually dived to the right at the end of its track instead of hitting into the pocket.

Depending on the way your ball rolls, the speed with which you roll it, and the amount of hook you are able to impart to it, the balance of your ball is very important in attaining strike action.

Earl Anthony rolls a semiroller ball. Here are the balances of the three types of balls he normally uses in tournaments. He calls them his strong, stronger, and strongest ball balances.

Strong	½-ounce side weight 1-ounce top weight
Stronger	½-ounce side weight ½-ounce finger weight 1½-ounce top weight
Strongest	1-ounce side weight 1-ounce finger weight 2½-ounce top weight

You must find out for yourself the best possible balances for your own strong, stronger, and strongest balls. You should consult the best ball driller in your vicinity and work with him to determine those balances. Once you have them, you are on your way to becoming a good bowler!

THE BOWLING BALL TRACK

It is easy to determine the ball track, or roll of the ball. This is the worn band around its circumference that shows where the ball rolls down the lane. As it rolls, it picks up some of the lane dressing, and the result is a clear band of wear around the ball.

If this band lies between your thumbhole and the finger holes, you are rolling what is called a full roller. It rolls over the entire circumference of the ball—really its equator—and is an excellent mixing ball, although it does not hook much at the end of its travel. The bowler who rolls a full roller uses practically no wrist turn on the ball release.

The semiroller, also called a semispinner, is one that shows a track an inch or two outside the thumbhole. It is also called

Bowling balls roll on various axes depending upon the finger and wrist action that has been imparted at the delivery. The ball track can be seen clearly by looking at the surface of the ball for a worn-in track. If the ball has a very small circular track well to the left side (for the right-hander) the ball is called a *spinner*. This ball will produce a large curve/hook and will cross a number of boards on its way to the pocket. The *full roller* rolls on what might be called the equator of the ball. It produces much less curve than the spinner. The *semi-spinner* ball is one that has its track about halfway between the rolls of the spinner and the full roller. It produces a strong hook and is the one used by most good bowlers as it is easier to control than the spinner and gives more power than the full roller. If your bowling ball shows an erratic track, you are not rolling the ball with consistent finger, hand, and wrist action.

a three-quarter roller because that is about the amount of ball surface in contact with the lane. The bowler who rolls a semiroller has a good hook, and his or her release combines the squeeze or lift and moderate wrist action as well.

The spinner ball is just what the term implies. Its track is way down on the ball and covers only a small part of the circumference of the ball. The ball spins down the lane much like a top. It does not have much mix or power. The spinner is rolled with a great deal of wrist turn at the point of ball release.

Your ball track can tell you how consistently you are delivering the ball. If the track is a narrow one, it shows consistency. If it varies several inches, it shows that you are not releasing the ball the same way every time.

Although it is interesting to consider the ball track and find out what kind of ball you roll, it is very difficult to change from one type of roll to another. There is something basic about the anatomy and musculature of every bowler that consigns each one to roll the ball in his or her own natural way. That way will turn out to be either a full roller or a semispinner most of the time with the same finger and wrist motion, whether with turn or without. Always make it the same and you are on your way to consistent delivery and to becoming a good bowler.

How to Throw a Straight Ball

It is relatively simple to throw a strike ball with action imparted by the easily learned squeeze. However, if you are having difficulty mastering this, you may prefer to throw a straight ball without the squeeze. Let your thumb point directly at the headpin and let the ball come off your fingers without any wrist turn or movement whatsoever, and without any squeeze action of the fingers. You will, of necessity, move several boards to your right and direct the ball straight into the 1-3 pocket. If you move to compensate for the lack of curve on the last few feet of your ball track on spares or splits, don't expect ever to be a good bowler. You may become a respectable bowler, perhaps average in the 150s, but your ball will be subject to such deflection that you will have more splits than the average bowler who throws a ball with the squeeze and its consequent action.

Bowl the straight ball from the right-hand side of the approach and slant directly in toward the headpin and the 1-3 pocket. Adjust your starting position according to the suggestions earlier in this book, moving with your error. The

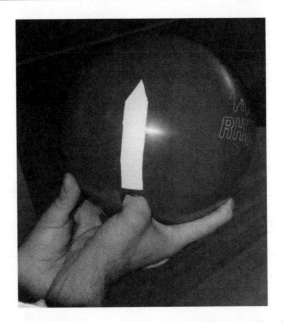

All the fundamentals of the bowling delivery apply to the delivery of a straight ball. The body must remain square to the line, but since the line for a straight ball is from the corner of the lane from Right Center Position or even from Far Right Position, the squareness of the body is toward a line directly into the 1-3 pocket. It is difficult to knock down a lot of pins with a straight ball because of the deflection of the ball at the pins, lacking power to get through and knock down the 5 pin.

body remains square to the line, but since the line for a straight ball is from the corner of the alley from Right Center Position or even from Far Right Position, the squareness of the hips and body is toward a line directly into the 1-3 pocket.

You will find it very difficult to throw a true "straight" ball. The wrist at the last second will give a slight turn one way or the other and the ball will either curve slightly left or back up right. Either way, you will find that it is difficult to knock down a great many pins because of the deflection of the ball. All the other fundamentals of bowling apply just as well to the straight ball—the timing, the relaxation, the firm wrist. Just don't squeeze!

_____ PART II

THE SECOND BALL

Basic Starting Positions

There are only five basic starting positions you need to know and use consistently in making strikes, spares, and splits.

Let's start with the most important one, Strike Position. Normally you will start with your left foot on the center dot of the approach. That brings your right shoulder in line with the strike line between the second and third arrows on the lane.

The second is Strike Position, Crossover Line. This starting position is used to take the ball into the 1-2 pocket, or the crossover spot. It simplifies making many of the spares which have the 1-2 combination standing. Presuming that the bowler has found that his strike line is down the 18th board, that is, the third board to the left of the third arrow, he will find that by rolling his ball one board to the left of that strike line his ball will cross over and come into the "Brooklyn" or 1-2 pocket.

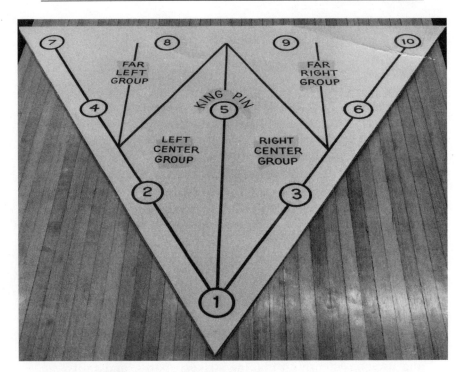

Study and memorize this diagram of the spare groups. It shows the pins, by groups, that control your starting position for conversion of each one in the most effective way.

Notice that there are two three-pin clusters—one on the right, the 6-9-10, and one on the left, the 4-7-8. They are always bowled cross-alley, from Far Left for the 6-9-10 and from Far Right for the 4-7-8.

There are two four-pin clusters—one on the right and one on the left. They are the 1-3-5-9 and the 1-2-5-8. Since they are more in the center of the pin setup they are bowled from Left Center for the 1-3-5-9 and from Right Center for the 1-2-5-8. If the 5 pin is in the cluster you should bowl for the 1-2-5-8 from Strike Position, pretending that you have a full 10-pin setup. If the 5 pin is absent you should use the crossover or Brooklyn line.

If you do not have a complete group (for example, the 9 pin might be absent from the Right Center 1-3-5-9 group), you will still bowl against the spare from Left Center. The same theory holds true for the 1-2-5-8 group if the 8-pin is not standing.

This diagram is intended to organize your spare shooting so that you will always know the best way to convert them by taking advantage of the ball track through the pins.

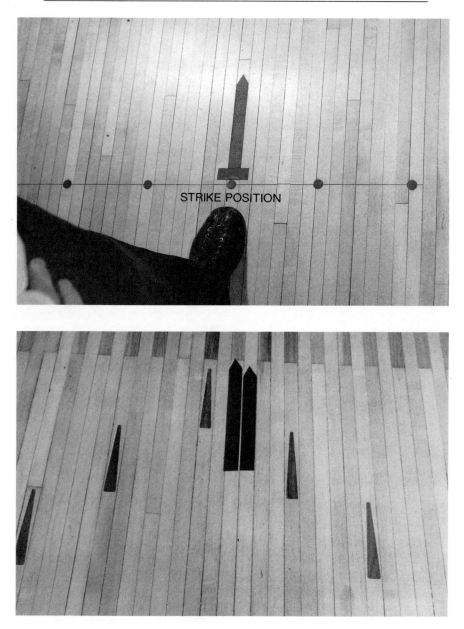

STRIKE POSITION

The right-hand arrow indicates your strike line. One board to the left of that line is your "Brooklyn" or crossover line, which will take your ball into the 1-2 pocket. It is useful for converting the 1-2-10 split as well as many other spares in the Left Center Group.

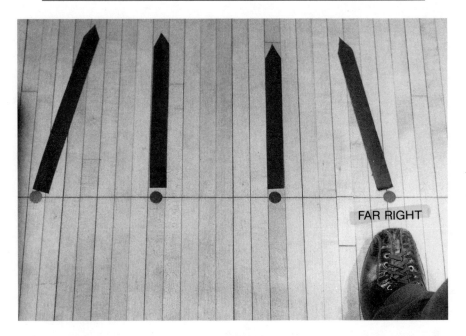

FAR RIGHT

FAR RIGHT STARTING POSITION

You will use the Far Right Starting Position to convert spares on the Far Left side of the lane. Place your left foot, your aiming foot, on the seventh board to the right of Strike Position and square your body to the line of your target at the break of the boards, the dart-shaped range finders 12 to 16 feet out on the lane. You will bowl on an angle directly across the lane.

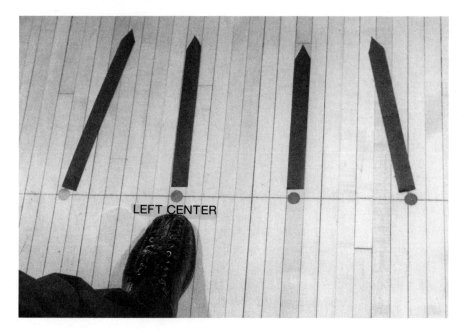

LEFT CENTER

LEFT CENTER STARTING POSITION

Place your left foot on the seventh board left of the center dot. Square your body toward the pins and the spare. This starting position is used for Right Center Group pins. If your spare happens to have pins from both groups—that is, the Far Right and the Right Center—the importance of getting the pins in the Center Group determines your starting position and requires that you start from Left Center.

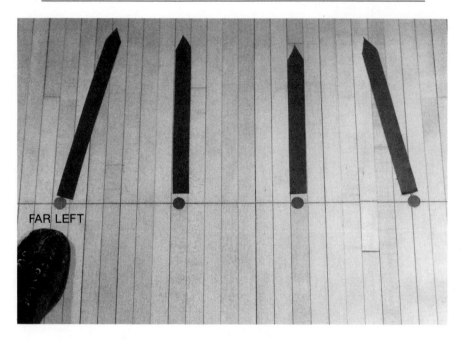

FAR LEFT

FAR LEFT STARTING POSITION

Place your left foot on the 14th board left of the center, or "strike," dot. Face directly toward the pins on the far right side of the lane. You will be definitely rolling cross-alley with this position. You must be aware, however, that since your ball will be delivered from the right side of your body, your actual delivery position will not be as far to the left as your Far Right delivery was to the right in making Far Left spares.

Let your arm swing directly toward the pins and do not let up on your speed lest your ball run away from you at the end of its travel. Be careful, too, to deliver the ball with your customary speed and finger action so that the ball doesn't fail to come up. You will use this Far Left Starting Position for Far Right spares.

How to Convert All the Spares

As we all know, it is impossible for a bowler to strike in every frame. When he does not, he has what is called a *leave*, one or more pins which must be knocked down on the second ball to "convert the leave" into a spare for a bonus of 10 pins.

It is very important that the bowler concentrate as much on his spare shooting as he does on rolling his first ball for a possible strike. So often an inexperienced bowler will get angry when he does not get a strike on his first ball and, as a consequence of that anger, will fail to concentrate on his second ball. He rolls it carelessly and misses. Such careless misses can cost a bowler many pins on his average over a season of bowling. I recommend that you resolve here and now never to roll a careless second ball. There's an old bowling expression, "Get the spares and the strikes will take care of themselves." It's true, too.

Most leaves can be converted into spares if you concentrate on them and bowl them from the best possible angle so as to take advantage of the ball track and pin action.

The secret to shooting spares and to converting splits is in knowing and understanding what each pin is supposed to do once the chain reaction of the ball hitting the pocket has been accomplished. The word *pocket* is being used loosely here. Much as the 1 pin and the 3 pin are the strike pocket, so, too, in the 2-4-5 spare, for example, the pocket is the 2-5. In the 6-9-10 leave, the pocket would be the 9-10.

Once you know the best way to convert spares your object is to aim your ball at the spot that will start the chain reaction you must have to help you get the other pin or pins and make the conversion. The following pages will show you clearly the secrets of successful spare and split conversions.

The Target Pin

In the heart of every spare you leave, there is one key pin that must be knocked down or split conversion will fail. This pin is called the target pin and, in many cases, if you really concentrate on hitting only that pin and ignore the rest of the pins that are standing, you will be successful.

Ordinarily, we are not talking about simple one- and two-pin spares when we talk about the target pin of a spare. We mean spares with three or more pins standing. One example is a 2-4-5-8 spare—the infamous "dinner bucket," one of the bowler's most dreaded spares. The mere fact that these pins have been left shows that the bowler's first ball had less action than it should have had. That alone puts fear in the bowler's heart as he or she confronts the 2-4-5-8 cluster. Was it loss of action, or was it just too much speed that carried the ball beyond the 5 pin? Was it incorrect angle?

"I have to get that 8 pin (the target pin in this case). Shall I move more to the right and try more angle on it? Shall I roll my normal ball from strike position, play it as a baby strike (with the 2-5 pocket acting as the usual 1-3), and get the 8 pin that way?" These are some of the things that the bowler considers as he or she rolls at the 2-4-5-8 spare.

You see only the 8 pin in your mind's eye. The 2, 4, and 5 pins are not standing there at all. You envision the ball following its customary track with its normal action at the end and aim to hit the 8 pin solidly on its right side. In this case, the difficult four-pin cluster has become a simple one-pin spare you feel you can make with your eyes closed.

You must constantly be aware of the target pin in the hard spares. Focusing on the target pin will help you avoid worrying about many difficult multiple-pin spare leaves and will help you be very successful in converting many otherwise frightening leaves.

When your teammates congratulate you on making the "Polish Cathedral," for example, you can smile at them and say nonchalantly, "What Polish Cathedral? All I saw was the 8 pin!"

Bowling at the 10-Pin Spare

There are two schools of thought concerning the best way to convert the 10 pin every time. One is that you should never change your basic ball delivery style; therefore, even if you flirt with the possibility of rolling a gutter ball, you roll your normal hook from the far left position at the 10 pin, aiming for an imaginary pin to the right of it (a ghost pin standing in the gutter, that is) and let your hook occur in its normal way to take out the pin.

Bowlers who adopt this style of 10 pin coverage have to be careful not to loaf in their delivery. If they do relax, the ball may hook too soon and miss the pin on the left. Extra speed is required, and intense concentration, too. There is an old bowling adage, "You should never miss a one-pin spare." See to it that you don't!

The other school of thought about converting the 10 pin is that the bowler should change his basic delivery style from the normal hook ball to a straight ball, canceling out the hook at the end of travel. In this delivery, of course, bowling from far left position, you open your hand at the foul line and keep your thumb at 12 o'clock and fingers directly behind at 6 o'clock position, "killing the ball" so that it rolls straight at the 10 pin.

I cannot tell you which style of 10 pin conversion you should use. You will have to experiment with both methods. But once you have decided on one or the other, do not change. Use it consistently or you will end up in mental confusion and suffer a lot of unnecessary misses.

The tendency among the professional bowlers of today, by the way, is to roll the straight ball at the 10 pin. Perhaps that method will work best for you, too.

The Spares

Even the best bowler isn't going to bowl a strike in every frame. Its crucial for every bowler to learn to pick up his spares. The series of photos and captions that follow illustrates each possible spare in the various groups. Study the pointers for each spare and keep these tips in mind while practicing.

The 6-9-10 Spare, Far Right Group

For the 6-9-10 spare, your starting position is Far Left. Imagine that this leave is a baby strike: plan to hit it in its right-hand pocket. Don't think about the 9 pin, because you will probably get it with the 6 pin while the ball goes on to take out the 10 pin. You should always try to make this on its right-hand side so that if you do make a mistake in your delivery and pull it, or if your ball runs away at the end as it sometimes does as it gets on into the pin deck, you still have a chance to make the spare in its left-hand pocket or, as bowlers say, on the outside. This is an easy spare to miss. Be careful with it!

The Far Left Group

The 4, 7, and 8 pins constitute the Far Left Group. Without exception, they should be bowled from Far Right Starting Position. Always remember to allow for the extra distance the ball must travel to get to the back row of pins: for that reason choose a line or spot slightly to the right of the line your eye tells you to use. You will find that you will miss this spare most often on the left-hand side because of your failure to make this suggested allowance.

The Left Center Group (with the 5 Pin)

For the 1-2-5-8 spare your start position is Strike Position. This cluster might just as well be the entire setup of 10 pins. The presence of the 5 pin is crucial here because just as it is the kingpin in the strike setup, it is the kingpin here, too. You must roll a ball with action to get this center group in order to power through and get the 5 pin. Even if you have the 4 pin or the 7 pin added to this spare you will still attack it from the Strike Position.

The Right Center Group

The 1, 3, 5, and 9 pins constitute the Right Center Group, and you will use Left Center Starting Position to convert these pins or nearly any combination of them. If you happen to have the 6 pin or the 10 pin as well, your best strategy is to remain in Left Center Starting Position in order to decrease your chances of cutting off—that is, leaving—one or more of the pins. If the 5 pin is present, you may have to experiment to determine for yourself whether you find it easier to convert this leave from Strike Position or from Left Center. Once you have made that determination, stick with it.

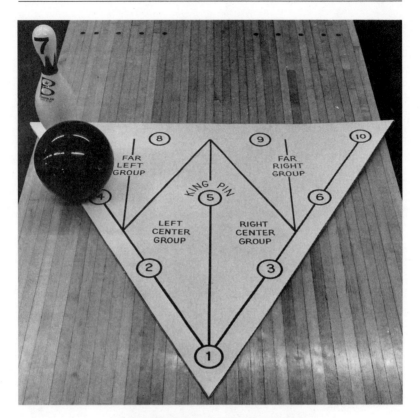

The 7-Pin Spare, Far Left Group

For the 7-pin spare, your starting position is Far Right. Because this
pin is so close to the channel, remember that your target is cut down
by about seven inches. Because your ball will be curving into the pin
rather than away as it does on the 10-pin spare, however, this spare
is easier to convert than the 10-pin spare, at least for the right-
hander. The opposite is true for the left-hander, of course. Be sure
that you don't ease up on this spare, or your ball may run away to the
left and cause you to miss it. Line yourself up squarely for a shot at
the right-hand side of the pin because that is where your greatest
margin of error lies. Go after it with authority. You should make this
spare every time.

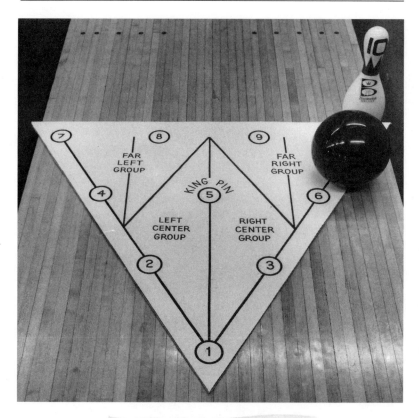

The 10-Pin Spare, Far Right Group

For the 10-pin spare, your starting position is Far Left. This spare is one of the most frequently missed easy spares in bowling. The 7 pin is equally as difficult for the left-hander. Since the 10 pin is in the back row of pins, your ball has a tendency to take off in its hooking action at the end, thus causing you to miss this pin on the left. On the other hand, if you speed up your ball you may lose some of your action and find that your ball falls into the channel short of making the pin. I recommend practicing this 10 pin by imagining a pin standing in the channel to the right. Shoot for it or find your own spot at the arrows which will usually take your ball through the 10 pin. Whatever you do, don't loaf on the shot. Be sure you follow through, because the least pull to the left will cause a miss. Always try to hit the 10 pin flush, and then you will have some margin of error if your ball acts erratically at the end of its track.

The 5-9 Spare, Right Center Group

For the 5-9 spare your starting position is Left Center. This leave will occur when you have a crossover hit on the Brooklyn side of the pin setup. It is a difficult spare because of your chances of picking off either pin and leaving the other. By bowling from Left Center you have the best angle at this spare. Be certain that you roll your ball a little harder than usual because the pins are farther back than usual and your ball may take off at the end and chop the 5 pin, leaving the 9 pin. You will have to experiment with this spare to find your own best method of making it. Moving your start a board or two to the right or left may make a big difference in your ability to convert it regularly. Everyone chops this (hits the front pin and leaves the other) once in a while, so don't get upset if you do, too!

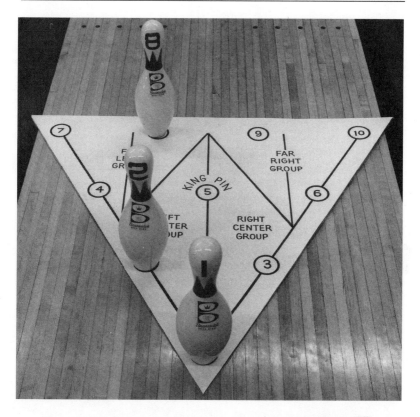

The 1-2-8 Spare, Left Center Group (Without the 5 Pin)

For the 1-2-8 spare, your starting position is Strike Position, Crossover Line. This spare and other spares related to it (like the 1-2-4-8, the 1-2-4-7, and the very unpleasant washout spare, the 1-2-10) are all bowled in exactly the same way, from Strike Position but over the crossover spot at the arrows. Most bowlers feel more comfortable when they bowl in their usual starting position, the strike position, so you should be very relaxed about this spare. Roll your normal strike ball at it, giving your ball normal action and finger lift, to make sure that you carry through to get the 8 pin. If you keep missing the 8 pin on the right-hand side on this spare, you need either more finger lift or more angle. On the other hand, if you keep missing it on the left, you should cut down on your angle by moving left at the start of your approach.

The 2-4-5-8 Spare, Left Center Group

For the 2-4-5-8 spare, your starting position is Left Center. This spare is one of the most dreaded that any bowler will encounter. Even when it is struck with an ideal spare ball, it seems that sometimes a pin will be chopped. I recommend treating this setup as a "baby" strike and moving to your left for your starting position. Bowl it straightaway—that is, as if it were a strike setup—and plan to have your ball come into the 2-5 pocket the same way you would normally come into the 1-3 pocket if it were a strike. Your ball must be rolled with action so that it carries on through to take out the 8 pin. If you get too high on the 2 pin your ball may fail to take out the 5 pin. Once in a while you may get lucky when you really have missed this spare and still convert it by bouncing a pin off the side wall (the kickback on each side of the pin deck) to take out a pin that would otherwise have been a cherry.

From the headpin to the 5 pin is 22½ inches. It is the same distance from the 3 pin back to the 9, or from the 2 pin back to the 8 pin. When you realize that the other pins, such as the 4, the 5, and the 6, are only one foot apart, you can see why it is easy for the ball to deflect off the front pin and miss the rear pin. The back pin is called a *sleeper*, and sometimes it is called the *mother-in-law*, for obvious reasons. Sleepers are difficult to convert. You should practice hitting them head-on with power so as to carry through the longer distance to the back pin.

Because there are only 2½ inches between the 10 pin and the right-hand channel, you do not have the advantage of the full width of your ball track on the right side of the lane. The same principle holds true, of course, for the left-hander shooting for the 7 pin. Your target on these two pins is about seven inches narrower than it would be for a single-pin spare standing in the center of the lane. Make sure that you use cross-lane angle on either of these spares, and make sure you hit them in dead center. The least variation on either pin on the channel side will cost you the spare.

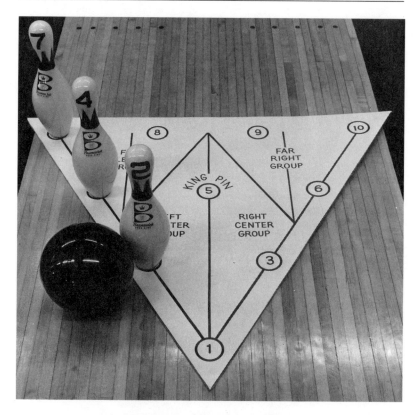

The 2-4-7 Spare, Far Left Group

For the 2-4-7 spare, your starting position is Far Right. Plan to hit the 2 pin on its left side and let the ball deflect into the 4 pin and continue on its way to the 7 pin. Even if the ball does not get all the way to the 7 pin, the 4 pin may help you by deflecting into the 7 pin for you and taking it out. You must take advantage of the cross-alley angle on this spare because if the ball comes in from the left on the 4 pin you may hit it too far on its right side and it may wrap around the 7 pin and miss it. Sometimes you may see this spare made by hitting the 2 pin on its right side and letting the 4 pin go on to take out the 7 pin. I do not recommend this because there is too much of a chance that the 7 pin may be left.

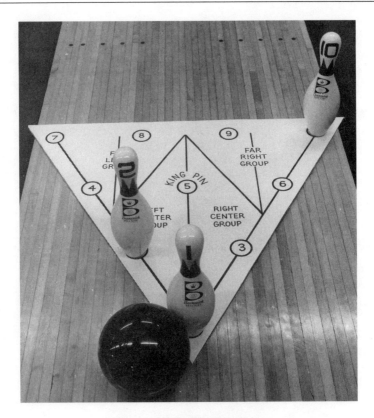

The 1-2-10 Washout Spare

For the 1-2-10 Washout Spare, your starting position is Strike Position, Crossover Line. You should be able to convert this spare without too much difficulty. Basically, it is the 1-2 spare you make comfortably by rolling from your strike position but over the crossover line, which takes your ball into the 1-2 pocket. The 2 pin, having been struck on its left side, is driven over across the lane to take out the 10-pin. This is a flashy spare to make and a very satisfying one. If you leave it very often, it is a sure sign that your ball is not getting to the pocket quickly enough. You may be lofting the ball out onto the lane too far, and your action may be starting so late that the ball gets in behind the head pin. You may also be rolling the ball too fast, thus cutting down on the ball action at the pocket. Be sure to roll your normal strike ball on your second effort. The crossover line should work to help you get the 10 pin regularly.

The 1-3-6-10 Spare, Right Center Group

For this spare, your starting position is the Far Left Starting Position. This is a wicked spare, one that is often missed even when it is apparently covered. Anytime you must count on pin action (motion of struck pins) to take out part of a spare, you run a chance of missing. The strategy here is to put your ball into the 1-3 pocket and then get some help from the 6 pin in taking out the 10 pin. If you move too far left for your start, you may end up with the ball sliding by the headpin and, of course, missing the spare. If you move too far right, you may just plain chop right through and leave the 10 pin standing as the 6 pin wraps itself around the 10. Sometimes this spare can be made by hitting the headpin on its left side and counting on pin action to take out the other pins down the line. Your best bet is to try for the pocket and get as many pins as you can with your ball and ball track. Don't be upset at missing this spare. Everyone misses it some time.

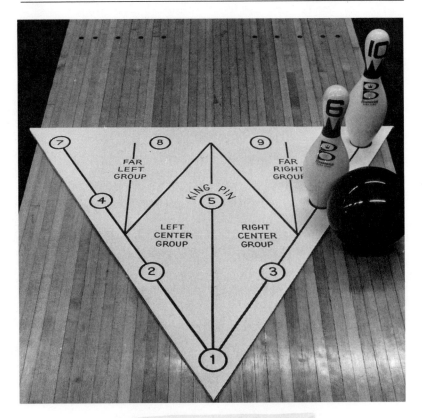

The 6-10 Spare, Far Right Group

For the 6-10 spare, your starting position is Far Left. Along with its counterparts, the 5-9 and the 2-5, this spare is a difficult one for the right-handed bowler because of the tendency of the curving ball to cut sharply through the front pin and take it off the other pin, which remains a "cherry," as bowlers call a pin left standing when a pin in front is chopped. I suggest that you bowl to make the 10 pin full because you will find that nearly always your ball will move slightly at the end of its track and get the 6 pin for you. This spare is great for 6-7-10 split practice, too. You will be able to tell whether you would have driven the 6 pin across the lane to take out the imaginary 7 pin.

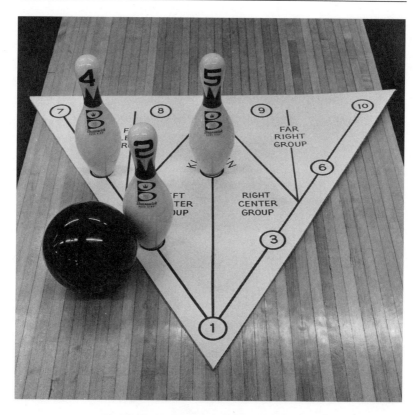

The 2-4-5 Spare, Left Center Group

For the 2-4-5 spare, your starting position is Strike Position, Crossover Line. This leave happens when your first ball is light in the pocket and never reaches the 5 pin. Because there are three pins, it is another one of those troublesome spares. It is easy to pick either the 4 pin or the 5 pin, depending on which way your ball hits the 2 pin on either its right- or left-hand side. Your best bet to convert this spare is to take the crossover line from your normal strike starting position and let the ball come into the 2-5 pocket as if it were coming into a full pin setup for the 1-3 pocket. This strategy is good, too, in case you miss the spare on the left-hand side, because your ball may yet cause the 2 pin to go to the right and get the 5 pin. If you keep leaving this spare frequently, it is an indication that you do not have enough action on your ball. You need more finger lift or more angle from the right to get the ball into the pocket.

The 2-8 Spare, Left Center Group

For the 2-8 spare, your starting position is Strike Position, Crossover Line. Bowl this one from your familiar strike starting position, but take the crossover line, which will cause your ball to travel through the 2 pin to take out the 8 pin. This spare is a very demanding one, and the slightest variation to the right or left will result in "picking the cherry"—leaving the 8 pin and missing the spare. The 8 pin is often called "your mother-in-law" for obvious reasons. This is a hateful spare because your ball must have enough power to overcome its tendency to deflect away from the 8 pin and thus miss it. Remember that the 2 pin is the same 22½ inches in front of the 8 pin that the headpin is in front of the 5 pin. Really concentrate on this spare and any others which have "sleepers"—pins hidden behind each other.

A Short History of Bowling

It is believed that pin bowling was introduced in America in 1623 by the Dutch settlers on Manhattan Island. The game, called ninepins, was played outdoors with nine pins and a ball. The nine pins were set up in a diamond formation and the object was to knock down all the pins with one throw.

Ninepins became very popular not only as a sport but as a bettor's game. The Puritans outlawed bowling because of the gambling connection. Later, in 1841, the Connecticut state legislature prohibited the game, and other states did the same.

Then an imaginative bowler figured out a way around the prohibition. He added a 10th pin. The game, renamed tenpins, quietly resumed and became more and more popular. By the middle of the 19th century the first indoor lanes were built in big cities such as New York, Syracuse, Buffalo, Cincinnati, and Milwaukee.

In 1895 the American Bowling Congress was organized in New York and the rules of the game were standardized. The game has remained basically unchanged except for the technological advancements brought on by the modern age. These include the introduction of automatic pin setters, plastics, and other synthetic materials.

We have to thank that daring bowler in the mid-1800s for adding the 10th pin to the triangular pin setup we bowl against today. That 10th pin has given the bowler fits ever since. No matter how perfect the hit into the 1-3 pocket, it seems that, most unjustly, the 10 pin, or the 7 pin or some other pin or pins, will remain standing.

Let's analyze what happens when the first ball rolled goes into the strike pocket (the 1-3 for the right-hander, the 1-2 for the left-hander). The ball strikes the 1 pin first, then the 3 pin, then the 5 pin (if it is strong enough to get to the 5 pin), and then the 8 pin or 9 pin. It then goes into the pit.

Note that the ball actually strikes only four of the pins. We have to rely on "pin action," kinetic energy, imparted to the other six pins, which must be struck one by one and toppled before we have all 10 pins down for a strike. Sometimes the ball appears to dive "under" the pins and send them flying in a spinning sideways fashion toward the other pins. Other times, the ball seems to merely part the pins in a vertical fashion, and although the other pins do fly toward one another they may cut a swath only 4¾ of an inch wide, the width of the pin. This causes the split, the one-pin tap, usually the 10 pin for the right-handed bowler and the 7 pin for the left-handed bowler.

We must reconcile ourselves to an occasional one-pin leave or a split. We must have the help of the flying pins in order to down all the pins. When they won't cooperate, no matter how perfect the hit in the 1-3 pocket with action on the ball which carries it through the 5 pin and the 8 pin or 9 pin, we have been "tapped."

The tap and the split are part of the game and must be accepted. We have to count as many spares as possible, convert as many splits as possible, and make up for the occasional open frame by following it with a double, a triple, or more strikes in a row.

Take an open frame as a challenge! Get a double immediately and you'll even the game.

Splits in Bowling

You have a split when two or more pins are left standing after a first ball and the space of a missing pin or pins between them makes it more difficult to "convert" or "make the split." Technically, under American Bowling Congress rules, if the headpin is left standing no split is designated. In my opinion, one of the most exciting conversions ever made is the 1-2-10 "washout" in which the bowler rolls his second ball into the left-hand (1-2) pocket so precisely that the 1 pin is driven sharply across the alley to take out the 10 pin. Since the headpin, the 1, happened to be standing, this conversion merits only a "spare" mark. I disagree with the ABC and believe that a special mark should be given for this conversion or, for that matter, for the conversion of any "wide-open" splits.

As you will find out by experience, or already know, there are moderately wide and "wide-open" splits. Wide-open splits are always those with two pins or more on opposite sides of the alley and in the same row, either the second row or the back row. These are so difficult to convert that they are usually called impossible. Once in a long while the ABC will award a special arm patch for the bowling shirt of anyone who has been accurate enough, or lucky enough, to convert the "big four," the 4-6-7-10 split, or you will hear of someone making the 4-6, the 8-10, or the 7-9. Sometimes this happens when one pin is hit so hard that it flies up into the rack or into the padding at the back of the pit and ricochets back into the alley to clear the other pin.

Some splits which at first glance appear wide open and impossible are, in actuality, possible because one pin is in the row in front of the other, usually called "fit-it-in-between" splits. Still other splits, referred to as "slide-it-over" splits, can be made by bowling at the front pin in such a way as to slide it over against the other pins and thus convert or make the split.

Study the following diagrams and pictures and learn to recognize the splits that are impossible and those that can be made with skill (and luck!), and your bowling enjoyment will increase immeasurably.

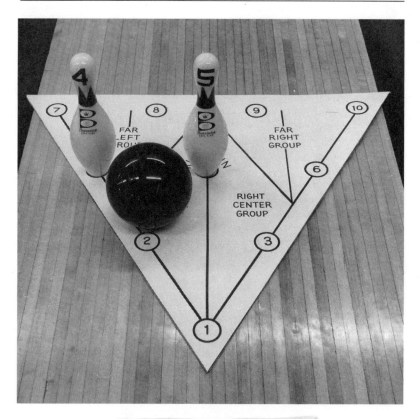

The 4-5 Fit-It-In-Between Split

Your starting position is Strike Position, Crossover Line. The strike position, crossover line, which takes your ball through the 1-2 pocket, will also enable you to convert this split with regularity. Sometimes it is useful to pretend that you have left only the 5 pin, that the 4 pin has fallen. Just roll the crossover line, hit the 5 pin thinly on its left side, and "accidentally" make the 4 pin as well. If you keep getting the 4 pin and missing the 5 pin, try rolling with a little more speed to delay your action at the pocket.

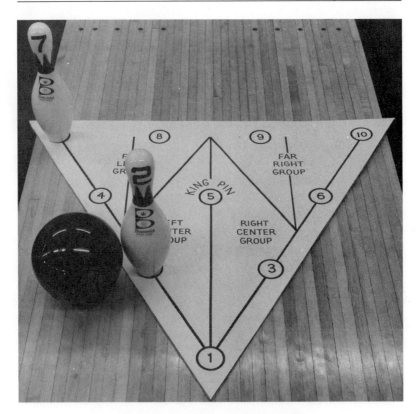

The 2-7 Fit-It-In-Between Split
(Also Known as the Left-Hand Baby Split)

Your starting position is Far Right. This split can be made from the outside, meaning that you strike the 2 pin on its right side and throw it into the 7 pin. I recommend that you convert it by striking the 2 pin on the left side and then letting the ball continue in its track to take out the 7 pin. It is easier for the right-handed bowler to make this baby split than it is for him to make the right-hand baby split, the 3-10, because his ball is curving into the 7 pin rather than away from the 10 pin as it is in the 3-10 conversion. If it helps you convert this split by imagining the missing 4 pin in the setup, by all means do so. You should practice making this split and the similar 3-10 so that you convert them regularly.

The 3-10 Fit-It-In-Between Split
(Also Known as the Right-Hand Baby Split)

Your starting position is Far Left. The counterpart to this split for the left-hander is the 2-7. It commonly occurs on a crossover hit into the 1-2 pocket and is a sign of an inaccurate first ball. There are several strategies you may consider using to convert this split. First, aim at the 10 pin alone and count on some movement left at the end of the ball track to catch the 3 pin. Second, aim to hit the "ghost pin," the missing 6 pin, flush and thus catch both the 3 pin and the 10 pin along the way, or aim to hit the 3 pin thinly on its right side and count on deflection of the ball to take out the 10 pin. Any way you attack it, it is a difficult split, especially for the bowler with a strong ball.

You have about 2 inches more in ball width than the distance between the pins. This split is the 5-6, but the same holds true for the
4-5, 7-8, or 9-10. These splits, along with the two baby splits, the 3-10
and 2-7, are possible to convert by fitting the ball between the pins,
hitting each pin, and knocking them both down. Remember your
spare angles and you can convert these splits regularly.

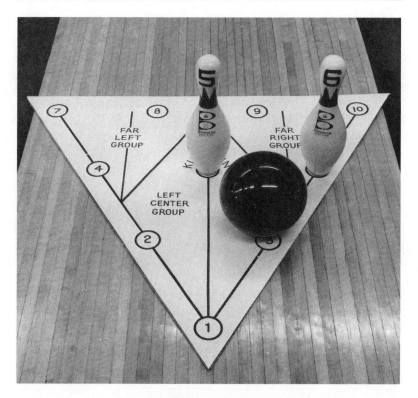

The 5-6 Fit-It-In-Between Split

Your starting position is Left Center. Though bowling from left center, remember to allow a little more to the right than your eye tells you because these pins are in the third row and your ball will be taking off in its curve in the last foot or so of its travel. This is a more difficult split to make than the 4-5 because you will have moved from your familiar strike position and your ball will be traveling on a line not frequently used and therefore of unknown characteristics.

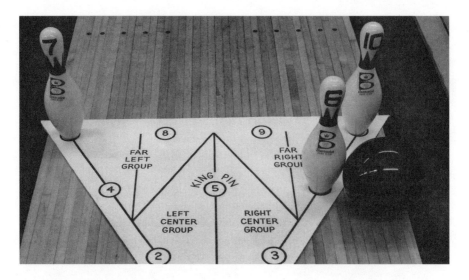

Although the wide-open splits are often termed impossible, if you look carefully at this 6-7-10 split you can see that if the ball is able to strike the 6 pin on its right side thin enough it may cause the 6 pin to slide over across the lane and take out the 7 pin. The same holds true for the 4-7-10 wide-open split, but that split is more difficult for a right-hander to convert because his ball is going away from the 4 pin while in the opposite split it is curving into the 6 pin. The reverse is true for the left-handed bowler: the 4-7-10 is easier for him than the 6-7-10.

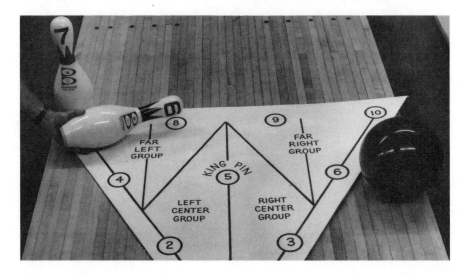

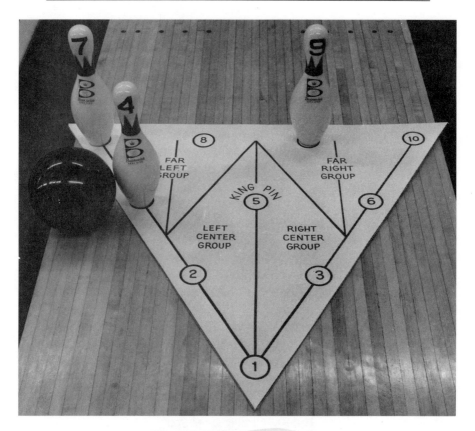

The 4-7-9 Slide-It-Over Split

Your starting position is Far Right. This split is bowled, and converted, in much the same way as is the 4-7-10 split. The difference, of course, is that the ball does not have to strike the 4 pin so thinly in order to get the 10 pin in the other split. This split is a warning to the bowler that his ball is coming in too high on the headpin. If you find that you are getting this leave often, change your angle so that your ball comes into the 1-3 pocket more toward the 3 pin. This split is easier to make than the 4-7-10 because the 9 pin is a foot closer than the 10 pin, so the 4 pin does not have to travel as far in order to take it out. You might have some success in making this split by pretending that the 9 pin is not even there and bowling for a thin conversion of the 4-7. You can make this split if you practice hard, but, again, be aware of possible loss of count if you do not make the 4 pin at all in your effort to hit it thinly.

The 5-7 Slide-It-Over Split

Your starting position is the Strike Position. There is a trick to making this split, and once you learn it you should be able to make it with regularity. If you will remember the discussion of the Strike Position, Crossover Line, you learned that by bowling from your customary starting position but over a spot one board left of your strike line, your ball would come into the 1-2 pocket for a crossover hit. The trick on this split is that instead of moving your line left at the arrows, you move it right one board and stay in your normal strike starting position. This move causes your ball to go out farther to the right and come into the pocket lightly so that it will strike the 5 pin thinly and force it over to take out the 7 pin. You must remember to throw your normal strike ball with regular action and don't ease up on the shot. It may be true, too, that you will have to adjust your spot a little more to the right at the arrows, but basically, this is the way to convert the 5-7 spare.

The 5-10 Slide-It-Over Split

Your starting position is Strike Position, Crossover Line. This split, along with the 8-10 split, is a sure indicator of a weak ball, one that has failed to get in to the 5 pin, one that has "died in the pocket." If you are getting this split or the 8-10 frequently, you are not getting the proper finger action on your ball. It is also possible that you should have an expert ball driller check the balance of your ball. You might need a stronger ball, one with more finger weight or side weight. You can convert this split by striking the 5 pin thinly on its left side and forcing it across the lane into the 10 pin. Try to make it from your normal strike starting position with the ball taking the crossover line, which will bring it into the 5 pin light. If you have trouble making this split from this position, try moving left a board or two from your normal strike position. You would then move your line at the arrows slightly left, too. Experiment until you find the best way for yourself. Once you find it, stay with it. It is a very satisfying split to make.

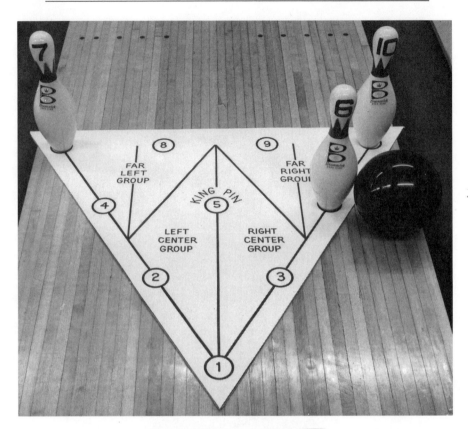

The 6-7-10 Slide-It-Over Split

Your starting position is Far Left. Aim for the 10 pin and attempt to hit it on its right side, even if you miss the 6 pin. Your ball will be snapping in strongly on the right-hand side of the 6 pin, which will be tossed over sharply across the lane to take out the 7 pin. Be certain to use sufficient speed on this shot, for the least bit of slowing down will spoil the shot as the ball may break too strongly into the 6 pin and cost you the conversion. It takes speed to impart enough power to the 6 pin to drive it across the lane. It is most discouraging to hit it with so little power that it travels partway across the lane and then fails to get the other pin.

The 4-7-10 Slide-It-Over Split

Your starting position is Far Right. Your strategy on this split is to strike the 4 pin thinly on its left side to slide it over across the lane and thus take out the 10 pin. It is a very delicate shot, and if the 4 pin is hit at all full, you just won't achieve enough angle to have it get the 10 pin. This split is considerably harder to convert than its opposite, the 6-7-10, because your ball will be running away from the 4 pin while it is running into the 6 pin in the other setup and helping it across the lane to do its work on the 7 pin. My own personal strategy on this split is to aim for the 7 pin and forget about making the split. Oftentimes, it happens that the hit on the 7 pin is so full that the 4 pin is clipped lightly on its left-hand side and forced across the lane for the conversion of the 10 pin. Try to convert this split only when loss of pin count won't hurt your team or your own individual match game. Most of the time it is best to get the two pins for sure and take advantage of the count.

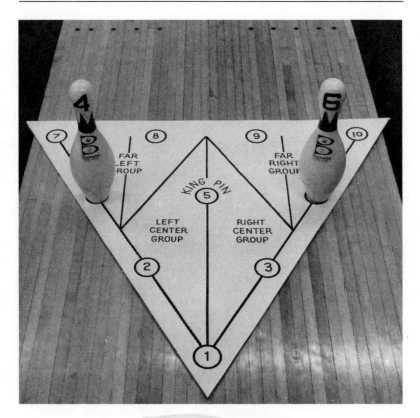

The 4-6 Impossible Split

This split, like the 4-6-7-10, will occur when your ball comes in too high on the headpin. In team bowling or other competition, work on your easiest pin to add to your count. If you are practicing, bowl at the pin you usually find hardest to convert. Practice hitting the 4 pin or the 6 pin dead on or on its left or right side as you determine, remembering that your skill at hitting either the 4 or 6 where you want it will add to your ability to convert the 4-7-10 or 6-7-10 split. You can even bowl at an imaginary 4-7-10 split or imaginary 6-7-10, and by watching what happens when you hit the 4 pin or the 6 pin, you can tell whether you would have made the split. Making it in your imagination is almost as much fun as it is in reality, and you will take the sting out of having had a split in the first place.

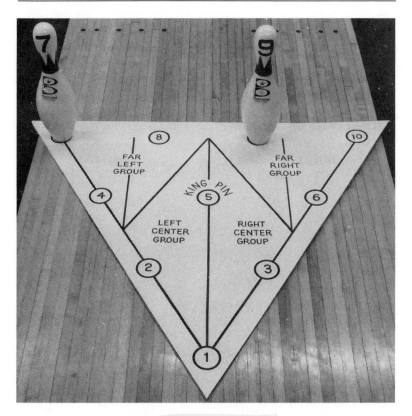

The 7-9 Impossible Split

Whenever you get a so-called impossible split, take advantage of the opportunity to practice on it. If you have been having trouble with the 7 pin, work on that pin. Experiment with your starting position by moving a board to the right or left from your normal Far Right starting position. You might try the same experiment on the 9 pin. Aim to hit either pin absolutely flush. That kind of practice will help your ability to make some of the more makeable splits when a pin must be hit precisely in order to force it to take out another pin. In league play don't experiment. Get your easiest pin and the greatest count possible.

The 8-10 Impossible Split

Your starting position is Strike Position, Crossover Line. This split usually occurs when your ball dies or flattens on a 1-3 pocket hit. It is a nasty split and a discouraging one because you have had hopes that you might get a strike. This split will pop up when your ball lacks proper roll. Possibly you overturned your ball, causing too much spin and not enough roll. Another reason might be that you did not use enough angle to the pocket and the ball deflected. Don't lose the opportunity to practice on the 10 pin if you are bowling in practice. You might even practice on the 3-10 split by imagining the 3 pin in front of the 10. If you are in competition, get your easiest pin for count.

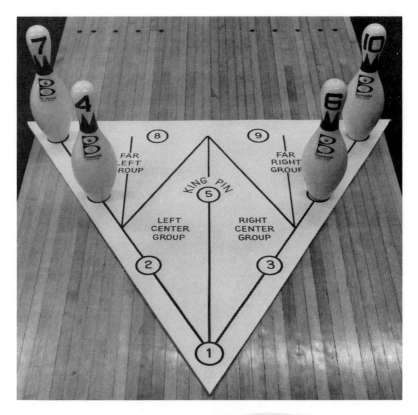

The 4-6-7-10 Impossible Split

This famous split, called double pinochle, is one of the most dreaded splits in bowling. It will happen when your ball goes in directly on the nose of the pin setup, usually without action. Be aware of loss of count if you do not convert at least two of these pins, so work on this split and get either the 4-7 or the 6-10. You can use this split to practice making the 4-7-10 split or the opposite 6-7-10 split. Once in a great while you may see the 7 pin or the 10 pin fall forward and come off the kickback (the side wall on each side of the pin deck) to take out the front remaining pin and actually convert this very difficult, if not impossible, split. There is great rejoicing when this happens, and the occurrence is so rare that the American Bowling Congress will award you a shoulder patch if you do make it.

The 4-6-7-9-10 Impossible Split

Although this leave is rare, it does happen sometimes when you might expect to have double pinochle alone. Oddly enough, it is more makeable (if any impossible split can be called makeable) than the 4-6-7-10: if you approach this split as if you were trying to make the 4-7-9 split, which we know is a Slide-It-Over and therefore makeable split, you may be able to throw the 9 pin into the left-hand side of the 10 pin and with luck have the 10 pin come off the wall and take out the 6 pin. I have seen this happen several times in my career, and it is sensational when it occurs. Make the 4-7-9 split out of this ugly cluster and hope for the best!

PART III

OTHER ADVICE, INFORMATION, AND SUGGESTIONS TO HELP YOU BOWL BETTER

Scoring, and Why You Must Always Take Advantage of the Count

In the early days of bowling the bowler rolled three balls in each frame. Later, when it became evident that the bowler was often downing all 10 pins in two tries, the frame was shortened to two balls, but a bonus of 10 points was awarded for knocking all the pins down in two tries. That is why, in the 10th frame, a bowler may roll three times rather than two. It's a holdover from ancient times.

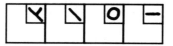

The scoring marks in bowling, from left to right, are strike, spare, split, and error or miss.

Scoring in bowling is not difficult once you understand the 10-pin bonus system. If you knock down all the pins with one roll of the ball, you have a strike, marked thus:

and you now get the total of your next *two* balls plus 10 points.

If it takes you two balls to down all the pins, you have a spare, marked thus:

and you get a bonus of 10 pins added to your *next single* ball. Note that after you have rolled a strike you wait until you have rolled two balls before you score the frame, while after a spare you wait for only one ball before you score the frame.

A strike followed by a spare or a spare followed by a strike always counts 20. The scoring looks like this:

Analyzing those scores you can see that with a strike "up" in the first frame, the bowler spared in the next frame, that is, knocked down all the pins and therefore scored $10 + 10 = 20$. In the second instance, the bowler with a spare up in the first frame knocked down all 10 pins with his first ball of the second frame. Therefore, $10 + 10 = 20$.

When you fail to knock down all the pins with both balls in a frame you total your count immediately. You have no bonus of 10 to carry over. You have had a "miss," an "error," an "open frame," a "failure to convert the spare." The scoring shows:

The latter mark is used sometimes when you "pick a cherry," that is, clip one pin off another in a spare cluster with more than one pin and you leave one pin standing.

The bonus of 10 is especially useful in the last two frames of a game. A strike in the ninth frame is called "laying a foundation" and allows the bowler the opportunity to "go all the way" in the 10th frame with three strikes in a row.

Here is an example of the scoring when a bowler strikes out in the 9th and 10th frames:

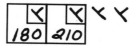

Now we will look at another score where the bowler does not strike out in the 10th frame. See the difference, a substantial one in "count" or total pins:

It is very important that you have a strike up and you split in the next frame to try to get as much count as possible. Let's say the bowler has a strike up and draws the dreaded "double pinochle" or 4-6-7-10 split. Carelessly, he misses all the pins on his second ball. His count is 16 pins, 10 plus the 6 he knocked down.

If he had knocked down two or even three of the pins in the

split his count would have been 10 plus 8 or even 9 for 18 or 19 pins total.

The moral is always try to get the highest count after a strike, even if you draw an impossible split. Many a game is lost by a single-pin margin. You will feel terrible if your team loses because you were careless and lost a lot of count.

You must always be aware of how you stand on the score sheet. Obviously, we try to fill every frame with a spare or a strike. An all-spare game with good counts will result in a high 180 game, even 190. You may even roll a "Dutch 200" game, with scores of spare-strike, spare-strike, spare-strike, spare-strike, and spare-strike.

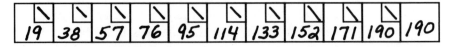

The score sheet of an all-spare game shows nine pin counts, no breaks, no strikes, but is still an excellent game.

As soon as you have an open frame, either a miss or an unconverted split, you must concentrate on getting two strikes in a row, a "double." It takes a double to offset the loss of count by an open frame.

Be aware, too, of the effect of several strikes in a row. For a 200 game (or a high 190 game) you need all marks plus a double. For a 210 game you need all marks plus a triple. If you don't get a triple, it will take two doubles, which equal a triple in count. For a 220 game you need all marks plus a "four-bagger," or four strikes in a row. Each double adds 10 pins to your score.

Many bowlers get nervous when they have a string of strikes going for them. When you have a double, try not to think, "I must get that third strike in a row!" Say to yourself, "I have a strike up. I'll try to get another one on top of it for another double." In that way you can keep the pressure off yourself.

The Language of Bowling

The language of bowling is changing with the passing years. Bowling proprietors are making every effort to change the public image of the sport from that of an unpleasant, smoke-filled hall full of carousing, beer-drinking men to that of a clean, healthful, family-oriented sport where women are also encouraged to participate and enjoy a few hours away from the cares of the home. Many bowling establishments today even have "sound rooms," glass-enclosed baby-care quarters so that mothers can bowl in mental peace knowing a trained baby-sitter is caring for their children.

Bowling alleys are no longer *alleys*; they are *lanes* nowadays. The trough on each side of the lane is no longer the *gutter* but is now the *channel*. Even the term *bowler* is turning into *player*, much as you have football and baseball players. The sport of bowling has a pleasant jargon of its own, and if you understand it well you will find that you can join the crowd in cheering or criticizing the bowlers around you. Knowing the language will make you more a part of the great game.

Most bowling terms seem to describe various types of bowling-ball "action." Rather than compile a dictionary, word for word, for you, I believe that there is a better way to acquaint you with the lingo. So here goes!

You have entered the bowling lane and one of your teammates laughingly tells you as you put your bowling bag down, "Don't get that water all over me!" He's merely referring to your bad night last week when you were throwing a *water ball*, a *pumpkin*, a *flat one*, or a *tomato*.

You proceed to bowl and your first ball is a slow curve that just barely comes up to the headpin, but once it touches it, all the pins start to dance and tumble down for a strike. Someone calls out, "You pulled the rug out from under that one!" or "You really stole that one," or "You're not going to take that strike, are you?" Soon after, getting up a little speed, you throw a strike on a ball that normally you expect to hook into or across the headpin, but it does not, and holds a direct line, and at the last moment seems to "set" and drives high and hard on the headpin for a strike. You come back to the bench and say, "Boy, was that a tight one! I was a little scared until it 'set!' " If all the pins flew backward, straight into the pit, without any question or doubt, you might say, "Was that a crasher!"

A "solid" hit is one right in the 1-3 pocket with such force and authority that usually a strike results. It follows that a *solid 10 pin* is one that is left standing after a *solid* smash. Don't be ashamed of *taps*, that is, leaving a 10 pin or a 4 pin or a 7 pin on what appears to be a good hit. A pin off-spot a fraction of an inch one way or the other, or erratic ball action at the last moment, can cause strange pin action and the loss of a strike that you might normally expect. Take your time and concentrate on converting the single-pin spare, for too many lone pins are missed merely because the bowler "blows the spare"—still rankling over the injustice of having left the single pin stranded on a good hit and forgetting to concentrate.

When you get your second strike in a row, you have "doubled"; you are now "working on a big one." When you get your third strike in a row you have a *turkey* or *triple*. More strikes in a row give you a *string* of strikes—one of the pleasures of bowling, especially when you get a lucky *Brooklyn* or *Jersey* hit in the opposite pocket, the 1-2 instead of the 1-3. You will hear more groans from the enemy and more encouragement from your own team as they say, "Don't be embarrassed—take it and sit down!"

Then come the splits! The *baby splits* are the 3-10, which a right-handed bowler draws frequently on a *high* hit, one that goes into the headpin too much toward the center; and the 2-7, usually drawn by the left-hander. The nasty 4-6-7-10, the two pins on each far side of the lane, is called variously *double pinochle*, the *Big Four*, or just plain *"Ugh!"* The 8-10 is called a *strike split* because it results from what seems to be a good 1-3 pocket hit. No matter what it is called, it's one of the impossibles.

Lanes, or alleys, are *running* when you can't hold your ball off the headpin, *stiff* when you can't make your ball curve and *come up* to the headpin. They are *soft* lanes when you regularly score well on them, *rough* or *tough* or *mean* when they are hard to score on.

There are a thousand more words and phrases you needn't know now. You'll learn them as you go along, and perhaps even invent a new one!

The Etiquette of Bowling

Bowling has a very old and well-defined code of etiquette which is observed by every knowledgeable bowler with good manners.

The first rule is that no one ever intentionally bothers another bowler while he is in the act of bowling, either by talking to him, by infringing on his territory on the lane, by shouting at him, or, in general, by any conduct which would tend to keep the other bowler from concentrating on rolling his ball down the lane.

An unwritten rule is that the bowler on the right-hand lane of a pair of lanes has the right-of-way to bowl first. In most cases he should proceed to bowl before the bowler on the left-hand side of the pair. Sometimes the privilege can be waived by the right-hand lane bowler. He merely indicates by a gesture that he would rather wait and let the bowler on his left proceed.

There is also an unwritten rule against "bowling into a split." No matter whether you are a right lane bowler or a left lane bowler, you do not want to bowl your frame until the

A very important rule of bowling etiquette is that you should never pick up your ball from the rack while another bowler is preparing to throw his ball down the adjacent lane. This is extremely distracting to the bowler, and you will feel as bad as he does when he delivers a "bad" ball.

other bowler has cleared his "mess" . . . a split. If you draw a split, get it out of the way as soon as possible and you won't run into the problem of this jinx for the other bowlers.

Never pick up your ball from the return rack while another bowler is preparing to bowl and is in his starting position. You may be out of his direct line of sight, but the movement of the balls on the rack may make enough noise to distract and upset him. If another bowler's actions consistently distract you, plan to take your time and let him have the right-of-way, even to the point of giving up your own right to bowl first at times. In that way you will remain relaxed and in control of your game.

If you are a team bowler you should always plan to be on time for the start of the bowling session. If you have to miss a night be sure that you let your captain know and that you have obtained a suitable substitute.

Good bowling etiquette calls for enthusiastic responses to your own good bowling and that of your teammates. Be happy when you get a strike and not too sad when you miss a spare or draw a split. Cheer the other bowlers' good play, too. Be a part of the team, a sparkplug, and you'll enjoy the game a lot more.

The Three Types of Modern Bowling Balls

In the early days of bowling, there were no finger holes in the bowling ball. The bowler "palmed" the ball and delivered it as best he could down the lane.

Finally, some bright person figured out that if the ball had a "handle" on it, it would be easier to control. He drilled some holes in the ball to fit his fingers, and the result was that the game was changed for the better. There are all kinds of drillings for the fingers now, including five-finger methods. On the whole, though, most bowlers find that using the thumb and the third and fourth fingers alone gives the best results in power and control of the ball.

For many years before the creation and use of plastics most bowling balls were made of lignite, an extremely hard wood, or hard black rubber. The surface of the ball was on the dull side but the ball gripped the lanes well and drove into the pocket satisfactorily.

Then came the introduction of the plastic bowling ball. At first just the outer cover was formed of a hard polyester. A few years later the whole ball was formed out of polyester.

The ball was made now in bright colors—reds, greens, blues—and the surface of the polyester ball could be controlled to a remarkable degree in the manufacturing process. For the first time the bowler could "tailor" his bowling ball to the lane conditions he faced. A very hard ball would skid farther than a soft one, so if the bowler found his ball hooking too soon on running lane conditions he could switch to a harder ball, which would skid a greater distance down the lane and then hook into the pocket.

The last few years have seen the rise in popularity of urethane bowling balls. Urethane is another plastic polymer, but it is chemically different from polyester and, to the delight of many bowlers, the urethane ball was most powerful at the 1-3 pocket.

Now there are three main choices of bowling ball available: the rubber, the polyester, and the urethane. There are other blends of several different materials, but for the purpose of this book we will consider those three choices and explain the benefits and detriments of their use.

For the beginning bowler and the good bowler who is just short of professional ability, the best ball is the rubber ball. It is considered a good all-around ball, that is, adaptable to all sorts of lane conditions. It comes in a range of soft and hard surfaces, so with some experimentation at your local lane and the counsel of your lane professional you should be able to find a ball that suits your bowling style and your own lane conditions.

The polyester ball can be made in degrees of hardness ranging from 75 to as much as 89. Your ball driller will use a scale called a *Durometer*, which gauges ball-hardness. The harder the ball surface, the more the ball will slide down the lane before hooking into the 1-3 pocket. Such a ball is useful on lanes that hook excessively. If you find yourself having difficulty holding the ball in the pocket, crossing over to the Brooklyn side frequently, it is probable that your ball is too soft, is grabbing the lane too much and too soon.

The urethane ball, which was brought out in 1981, has truly taken the professional bowling world by storm. Urethane had been introduced some 15 years earlier as the lane surface of choice, for consistency and longer wear without breaking down under intensive play. It made a lot of sense to manufacture a ball of the same substance as the lane surface. The result was a ball that tracked more smoothly and, best of all, hit the pocket with increased power when it did make its final "snap" into the 1-3 pocket.

The decision of which bowling ball to use is strictly up to you and your professional teacher. I recommend that you start out with the all-around good performer, the rubber ball. When you have learned to control it, are able to convert most of your spares, and a get a good percentage of strikes, then consider experimenting with a "stronger" ball such as the urethane.

Remember that the stronger a ball is, the more difficult it is to control. You may find that you may get three or four smashing strikes in a row with the urethane ball and then leave two or three wide open splits when the ball jumps into the headpin too soon or crosses over and leaves you an awkward spare to convert.

Keep in mind that the object of the game is to score the greatest number of pins. The old slogan "It isn't how, but how many," applies to bowling as well as to golf. A game with all spares will give you a score in the high 180s. A game with several smashing strikes and a lot of splits may give you a score in the 150s.

The important thing is that you understand how the various types of ball will react on the lanes. Make an intelligent choice as to the ball, or balls, you should use to give you the highest possible scores.

Exercises for the Bowler

To bowl your best at all times, you should be at your highest level of physical fitness. You have made a commitment to excel at bowling. You must also make a commitment to attain the best possible physical condition in order to achieve your goal.

Your body is made up of many different parts, all of which should be brought as close to optimum physical shape as possible. You need to be slim and lean so that you do not find yourself carrying unwanted pounds into the late games of a long series, thus contributing to a weariness that might sap your ability to roll the ball at your usual speed. There is an expression in racing that fits the situation: "I don't care how fast I come out of the chute; I just want to finish first." It is absolutely necessary, therefore, that you examine your stamina, your staying power. I am sure you will agree that no matter how impressive your stamina is at the present time, it can and should be improved.

If you are overweight, decide how many pounds you need to lose to get into good shape. I recommend that you do this in a sensible fashion by resigning yourself to altering your eating habits for the better, rather than by going on any crash diets. Ask your family physician to give you a balanced diet that will slowly but surely reduce your weight to the level you want to reach. Throughout the diet, eat carefully, drink alcohol moderately if at all, and lead what is called a regular life with a consistent routine of exercise, work, sleep, recreation, serious bowling, and bowling practice. Once your weight is under complete control, resolve to maintain it at that level for the rest of your life.

All good bowlers need strong legs. Your legs, especially the sliding leg, suffer a good deal of shock on every bowling delivery. It is not uncommon for bowlers to feel muscle strain in their legs and, of course, in their arms, shoulders, and back. The exercise program you develop should pay particular attention to increasing the tone and strength of the muscles in your hands, arms, legs, shoulders, and back.

JOGGING, WALKING, AND BICYCLING

Try a jogging program to strengthen your legs and your overall physical condition. Progress gradually, starting with a brisk walk and jogging half a mile or a mile a day, and slowly increase the distance until you can run from two to six miles a day without strain. Watch your pulse rate carefully, and in a few weeks you will find that your resting pulse rate is getting lower and lower, a most desirable effect because it indicates that your body machinery is working more efficiently.

If you do not like to jog—and many people find it boring, monotonous, even unpleasant—by all means find a substitute exercise that will provide the same results as jogging. Try walking at least two miles a day at a rapid pace and then increase your distance to three or four miles. While walking is not as rigorous an exercise as jogging is, it will give you the final result you seek: better leg power, better wind, and a better overall physical condition.

Another alternative to jogging or walking is bicycling.

Find the type of exercise you like and can live with from day to day, and indulge in it on a regular basis. Keep a daily chart of your achievements in distance traveled and in time elapsed. Set goals for yourself in distance and time, always striving for better results.

STRETCHING

Tension leads to stiff joints, aches and pains, and restricted blood circulation. Stretching exercises will help you lessen the tension in your body and avoid postbowling stiffness in your bowling shoulder, your bowling arm, and your legs.

Stretching exercises should be done in a relaxed manner and carried out intelligently. By no means should you push and pull your body through various extended positions, gritting your teeth in pain. This will hardly relieve your tension. Such a program might lead you to think you are making progress as your body adapts to the daily stretching, but this sort of program actually puts you one step backward every time you take two steps forward. It is a painful approach and sets up inhibiting psychological reactions.

The best way to achieve suppleness is to consider the program as three parts of relaxation and one part of stretching. If you ask your body to become more supple, it will, but you must cajole it. Here are some excellent guidelines on effective ways to urge your body to stretch.

1. You are your own director and stretching expert. You don't need to ask anyone else where and to what degree you need to stretch, because your own body, and your own mind inside that body, will tell you what to do and how far to go without undue strain.

   Whenever you feel tight, simply relax into a slightly more extended position than you are used to whenever you feel tight. That may sound too simple, but that's all there is to it. Feel where you are tense—your neck, your shoulders, your legs. Breathe deeply and imagine that your breath is moving out of your lungs and directly into the tight area, where it will loosen the knots of tension.

2. Stretching should be a good feeling, and once you practice it you will find it is good. Picture a cat stretching after a nap. Become a human cat, slowly, pleasantly stretching your muscles.

3. Stretch for only three or four minutes at a time and do so twice a day, once in the morning and once in mid-afternoon. Two daily sessions are more effective than one 10-minute session a day. Remember to be nice to your body. Don't force anything, but stretch smoothly.

4. Stretch when your body is warm, not cold. It's easier, it feels better, and it does your body more good when you're warm. This might mean that you schedule one of your stretching sessions after a warm morning bath and the other after an evening shower. You will probably feel that this will lead to more frequent baths, but this will also help you along the road to physical fitness, even bodily perfection. Don't stretch when you are cold. You may pull a muscle and set yourself back until it heals thoroughly enough for you to continue the program.

5. Stretch any way that you feel provides the results you want. Experiment with various moves and find the ones you like. Record them mentally or even physically in a notebook and build your own personal set of stretching exercise routines.

ISOMETRIC EXERCISES

Used regularly, isometric exercises are a marvelous way to improve your overall physical condition. When specifically directed toward the muscles used in bowling, these exercises will eventually help you improve your bowling.

I highly recommend isometric exercises. I was unable to handle the full fingertip ball because of insufficient finger and wrist strength, but after a whole year of studious isometric exercises such as those described here, I was able to use the fingertip ball most successfully for the rest of my bowling career.

Isometric exercise is defined by *Webster's Third International Dictionary* as exercise that "takes place against resistance without significant shortening of muscle fibers and with marked increase in muscle tone." Isometric muscle contractions, therefore, are those in which the muscles neither shorten nor lengthen, but only contract. In isometric exercises you don't move your joints and you don't move a load. The load involved in the exercises is solid, anchored, steady, or too heavy to move.

A typical exercise done by a weight lifter is the bench press. The lifter lies on his or her back on a bench, lifting and lowering weights with the arms. Each time he or she lifts and lowers, every joint in the arms and shoulders must be moved by the muscles in order to lift and lower the load. Suppose the weight is immovable. The exerciser exerts the same amount of effort against the weight, but it doesn't move. The joints don't move at all. Only the muscles contract. The harder the weight is pushed, the farther the muscles contract.

The contractions are hard to detect by anyone who might observe you carrying out an isometric exercise program. It is the perfect kind of exercise for you to do wherever you are—in your car, in your office, or while watching television in your living room.

The degree of each muscle contraction is completely at your discretion, and only the muscles you choose to exercise get a workout. The experts tell us that if you can hold a full contraction for seven to ten seconds you will gain strength in that muscle. Furthermore, the experts also believe that a very few isometric exercises per day are required to attain maximum improvement. That makes the isometric exercise program simpler and easier than other exercise programs that require considerably more physical activity, and yet as successful in the final results as any other type.

Isometrics do not replace your regular exercise program but should be added to it. Incidentally, you don't have to go through a warm-up procedure for isometrics. You warm up for an isometric exercise by applying only 50 percent of the muscle contractions you will eventually apply. That's all.

HOME ISOMETRICS

The following isometric exercises are meant to be performed in private, in your recreation room or bedroom. On each of the following time yourself by counting seconds: "One thousand and one, one thousand and two," and so on, to one thousand and seven, for a total of seven seconds.

The Arm Curl

This exercise is meant to develop and firm the biceps. Clasp your left hand firmly in your right hand, with your palms together. The left arm is extended down and across the body while the right hand is held near the right hip with the elbow flexed slightly. Flex the right arm upward as hard as you can while you apply equal downward pressure with the left hand. Do this both ways—left hand to right, right hand to left—to give both arms a balanced workout.

The Back Arm Lift

This exercise will develop and firm the triceps, the muscle on the back of the arm. Place your left arm behind your back and grasp it tightly with your right hand. Keeping your right elbow straight, lift your arm up and away from your back as your left arm resists the pull. Alternate arms but emphasize your bowling arm, of course.

The Hooked Finger-Pull

This is an excellent exercise to strengthen your shoulders and upper back. Hook your fingers together in front of your chest with your arms a little lower than shoulder height. Pull outward with a steady pull.

The Arm Press

This is the opposite of the Hooked Finger Pull. It will strengthen your chest, back, and shoulder muscles. Join your hands together a little lower than shoulder height. Push equally hard against both hands to reach maximum pressure and contraction. Experiment to find the best hand placement for you, but be careful not to strain your wrist.

The Hand Press

Here's a good exercise to strengthen and develop the muscles of the forearm. Holding both hands in front of your body, make a fist with your left hand and insert it between the third and fourth fingers of your right hand. Your right-hand fingers should be curved toward you. Press down with the fingers of your right hand while you bring your left fist up to counteract the pressure.

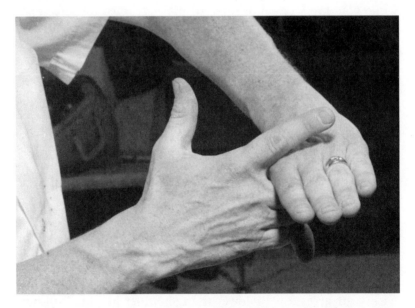

To properly strengthen your lifting fingers and your wrist by using isometric pressure, hold your third and fourth fingers firmly and press up on your left hand, which offers the resistance, for a count of seven seconds. Do this exercise five or more times in a row. It really works to give you the strength to manage a fingertip ball.

The Shoulder Hugger

This exercise will strengthen your shoulder and back. Cross your arms in front of your body a little above your waist. Give yourself a big hug.

The Shoulder-Hugger Squeeze

While doing the Shoulder Hugger, move your arms up to just below your armpits. One arm will have to cross over the other. The top arm should grip the back of the arm that is holding the side of the body. A big squeezing hug will give the muscles in the shoulder and back a real workout.

The Sit-Up "V"

You don't need to be told how to do this one. Lying on the floor with knees flexed, raise your trunk about halfway toward your knees and hold that position. Straighten your legs with your toes pointed and lift them from the floor to the same angle your trunk makes with the floor. Your body will now be in a V position with your buttocks at the base of the V. This is a great exercise for strengthening your abdominal muscles.

The Arm Pushaway

This exercise will strengthen the muscles of the shoulders, back, and arms. Stand in the center of a doorway with your feet wide enough apart to give you a solid base. With your hands at shoulder height, place them against the inside of the door frame and attempt to push the frame apart.

The Leg Push-Apart

This is good for strengthening the upper and lower leg muscles. It is related to the Arm Pushaway. Position yourself on the floor so that the area of your lower legs just above your ankles is against either side of a doorway. With your legs spread apart against the door frame, try to spread them farther apart against the resistance of the door frame.

The Hamstring Exercise

There is a great way to exercise and strengthen the hamstring muscles of the legs. Lean against a wall with your arms at shoulder height and gradually move your legs backward away from the wall while you attempt to maintain a straight body position.

Practicing Lift at the Line

To practice the action of the lift at the line, find an open doorway and put your body into the bowling delivery position with your hands clenched in the pre-squeeze position. Push with your hand, wrist, and arm against the side of the doorway for seven seconds. This exercise will also strengthen your forearm. If you perform it every day, it will work wonders for you.

The Bowling Ball Bag Exercise

Take your bowling ball bag and swing it forward and backward as you assume the same position you would have at the foul line making a delivery of the ball. Keep your eye on an imaginary target in front of you and concentrate on following through with your arm and shoulder. This is a wonderful exercise to use when you are away from the lanes and cannot practice as you usually would.

Explosion Point

I would like to call your attention to one final isometric exercise I have developed for my own use in the home. I firmly believe it will help improve your bowling style more than any other exercise. I call it the Explosion Point, and if it worked for me it should work for you.

To perform it, place yourself in a doorway (or up against a wall) so that the edge of the door is opposing your right hand and arm. Put your left foot in a straight sliding position at the doorsill and put your entire right arm, right hand, and wrist up against the right-hand side of the door.

Keep your hand in the squeeze position and push against the door. Make sure that the line from your fingers to your shoulders is perfectly parallel to the floor and that your body is squared to the imaginary bowling line. Your hand and wrist should be close to your sliding foot, and you should have a feeling of squareness to your line. You are rehearsing the perfect bowling delivery position.

OFFICE AND CAR ISOMETRICS

Several other isometric exercises can be performed while you are at work, in your car, or in your living room watching TV. In fact, the more you experiment with isometric exercises the more you will come to enjoy using them and especially enjoy the beneficial results that come from regular use.

The Wastebasket Squeeze

Most of us have wastebaskets near our desks. Keep your basket in front of you, and every time you use the phone put the inside of each foot against the outside of the basket and squeeze. This exercise will strengthen your leg and groin muscles.

The Finger Press

Take your left hand and hold it palm down. Press down hard on the third and fourth fingers of your right hand as they are clenched in the delivery or squeeze position. You can do this exercise a number of times a day at work or in your car while waiting for a traffic signal. It is a great exercise for finger, hand, and wrist strength.

The Desk Lift (Hands)

Put your hands under your desk and attempt to lift it from the floor. Practice putting your hand in the squeeze position at delivery and lift straight up, applying resistance to the clenched third and fourth fingers of your bowling hand.

The Desk Lift (Legs)

While you are sitting in front of your desk, hook your feet under it and attempt to lift it with your ankles. This exercise will strengthen the thigh muscles in the front of the legs.

Ball Squeeze

Keep a rubber ball with you at all times and practice squeezing it. With the ball in the palm of your hand, and your

Judi is practicing her squeeze technique with a little rubber ball. She holds her fingers open and relaxed, and then as fast as she can she closes her fingers in a firm grip simulating the action she wants when she delivers the ball out over the foul line. Notice that this exercise also rehearses the quick thumb release.

fingers relaxed, suddenly clench the third and fourth fingers tightly around the ball. Hold it for seven seconds many times a day. Each time you use the telephone you should remind yourself to carry out this exercise. For greater finger strength it is obviously one of the best exercises a bowler can do. Keep another rubber ball on the seat of your car and do the squeeze at every red light.

The Steering Wheel Crusher

To strengthen your arms, chest, and shoulders, use your steering wheel as your resistant point. Try to compress it from the 3 o'clock and 9 o'clock positions. Sit back until your arms are fully extended.

The Steering Wheel Pull

Using the same position as in the Steering Wheel Crusher, try to pull the wheel apart. This is a great exercise for firming the backs of the arms and developing the chest and back muscles.

The Steering Wheel Bowler Squeeze

As you wait for a traffic light, put your bowling hand into the squeeze position and pull up toward your face on the upper edge of the steering wheel. This will not only improve your hand and wrist strength but will also strengthen your abdominal muscles.

Developing Your Own Style

You have been told rather definitely to put your left foot here or there on a particular spot. Some people take longer or shorter steps than others, so it is entirely possible that your starting position should be from 6 inches to a foot or more in front of, or even behind, the particular dot you have been told to start from.

The best way for you to determine your starting position distance away from the foul line is to start at the foul line and walk away from the lane. With the heel of your shoe an inch or so from the foul line walk away from the line in what would be your normal walking steps. Note where your last step ends, add a half step to that point to account for your slide at the line, and you have your starting position within a few inches.

Don't be afraid to change your starting position moving closer or farther away from the foul line as you go along and your game develops. The closer you start to the foul line (at the three-step delivery spot, for instance) the more compact your delivery will be, and consequently there will be less chance of error in your approach. However, some bowlers find that they cannot develop enough speed on the ball from the three-step delivery spot.

If you find you need to use the entire length of the approach to be comfortable in your delivery, by all means, do so. Marshall Holman goes so far as to let his shoe hang over the edge of the approach to give himself that last inch of run toward the line.

Be sure to watch the great bowlers of the Professional Bowlers Association Tour in their televised matches now running on the ABC network, the longest running sport show in history. Notice the different starting styles of these bowlers, some traditional and classic, some with individual peculiarities. Wayne Webb dangles the ball back and forth until he senses the right moment to go. Notice the bad footwork of Marshall Holman, zigging in and out, on his way to the line. There are many bowlers who have succeeded in spite of glaring faults in their approach. All of them reach the line in perfect balance and rhythm and follow through the shot perfectly in most instances.

Experiment with your starting position and find the one that is best suited to your rhythm, tempo, and speed of footwork. Remember that you want to reach the foul line with your footwork in perfect synchronization with your armswing so that you are in excellent balance at the line and able to deliver the ball out over the line with authority.

After you have begun to standardize your bowling delivery and can count on 6 inches or more of hook at the end of your ball track, then you can depart moderately from the exact orders I have given in this book. But nearly all the starting positions I have set up for you remain valid in relation to one another and in relation to the various angles which are recommended for the conversion of the spares or splits. However, if you find that you can convert the 10 pin, or for that matter any other pin or spare, by going completely contrary to the recommended angle (that is, by bowling for the 10 pin from Far Right Position, as an example), by all means bowl for that spare from the angle you have found. The purpose of this game is to knock down the most pins, convert the most spares and splits, and thereby get the highest total score.

Some people simply cannot walk a straight line. You may be one of them. If you find that you cannot do it, it may be that the starting positions I have suggested for the straight walker are all wrong for you. Again, I say, "Experiment!" Understand the theory and put it into practice, adapting the various suggestions to fit your own individual bowling style.

Practice

AT THE LANES

Practice intelligently every time you do practice. Don't ever bowl for fun if you are seriously considering becoming a champion bowler. In my opinion, bowling for fun means rolling the ball at random targets without concentrating on your target line, your footwork, or your timing. If you get into the habit of bowling for fun with other people who distract you from your primary purpose, you will halt any progress you may have made toward bowling perfection. You may even take steps backward, losing the talent you have already developed.

I do not maintain that you should never bowl merely for recreation, but I do insist that when you bowl in circumstances that do not demand your best scores you should not lose sight of your eventual desire for perfection. You must concentrate on every shot you make and even use the distractions that are present—such as bad form exhibited by other bowlers or extraneous noise—as a testing ground to help you

improve your ability to concentrate under difficult circumstances.

When you practice, do not practice haphazardly. Always
have one or more goals in mind as the main object of a
particular practice session. Let me suggest a few thoughts to
you on practice methods that have worked for many bowlers
who have mastered the game over the years.

The most important thing about every practice session is
that you make sure you are rolling the ball properly. Therefore, the first few deliveries you make in a practice session
should always be with a view to observing the efficacy of your
timing and the consistency of your delivery. Are you delivering the ball out over the line so that you achieve your customary good roll on the ball? In other words, if you usually put
the ball down from 12 to 14 inches out over the foul line with
what is called moderate loft, you should be sure you are
placing the ball at that distance, not short of it or beyond it.
Once you have assured yourself that you are in normal form,
you can start to work on the goal of that particular practice
session.

Let us say that you have been having trouble converting the
5-7 split. With the advent of automatic pin setters with full
tenpin settings, you would think that it might be difficult to
practice making just the 5-7 split. This is not so. On the first
ball of your practice frame, merely move to the left and
practice making the right-hand baby split, the 3-10. You will
find that more often than not the 5 pin and 7 pin will still be
standing after your first ball has taken out the 6 and 10 pins.
You will have a few other pins left as well, but ignore them.
You are working on the 5-7 split only. On your second ball of
the frame, you have a practice shot at the split.

Whether or not you can use the practice method will de-
pend to a great extent on the type of ball you roll. It may be
necessary for the strong bowler to work first on only the 6 and
10 pins, in order to make sure to leave the 5 pin for the second
ball. My point is that you should experiment. Find out what
works and what does not work for you. Determine exactly
how far you need to move to the left of your usual starting

position in order to cause your ball to come in lightly on the 5 pin and snap it over to the 7 pin every time. You may need to move a board to the left, or two boards left of your usual starting position. It may even be necessary to move your target spot at the darts one board to the right of your usual spot.

As you practice making the 5-7 split, keep an accurate count of the number of times you convert it. Eventually you should build your odds of making the 5-7 split conversion to at least 50 percent. I have known good bowlers who will bet even money that they can convert the 5-7. They will take your money from you because they do convert it more than half the time!

A metronome is an excellent aid in perfecting your timing. The bowling delivery should be as smooth and rhythmic as a dance step. Another excellent idea is to use a stopwatch to time your bowling delivery. Ask a friend to help you. Have a notebook in which to record your performance. I suggest that you time 10 different successive bowling deliveries and then compare the times for each. Several segments should be timed separately. First, have yourself timed from the moment you take your starting position at the line. That interval is the first to examine for consistency.

Time yourself from the instant of your first move toward the line up to the explosion point as you deliver the ball out over the line. You may be one of those fortunate individuals for whom the first moves by hand and foot occur at the same time, or you may be one of those who starts with the hand or the foot first. It does not matter. Start the clock with that first move toward the line, whatever it is.

You should get a third set of figures, as well: the time it takes for your ball to travel down the lane to the pocket. You will find that time interval useful in speeding up or slowing down your ball at a later time.

At first you will find that there are inconsistencies in these various time intervals. But after a while you should be able to standardize the intervals until they become as automatically consistent as your breathing. Don't hurry, and don't make yourself overly self-conscious about it. Set your own pace, and once you have found it, don't vary it. You may find it useful to count to yourself, "One thousand and one, one thousand and two, one thousand and three," and so on, as you establish the rhythm you want in your bowling delivery when you take your ball from the rack and assume your starting position. If you carry out this practice regularly, you will find that the counting becomes unnecessary since you have established your routine and set it once and for all in your own determined rhythm.

Use a stopwatch to observe the present stars of the bowling world on national television. If you time one bowler in successive frames you will notice consistency in all respects of the pro's game, from the time to get set at the line to the time elapsed between the first move and the delivery at the line. You will also note variances of several seconds from bowler to bowler. It might be wise to imitate a bowler whose style and tempo seem to fit your own. In the long run, of course, you will work out your own individual timing and general style.

I recommend that you find one particular bowling lane in your vicinity and turn it into your regular practice arena. It need not be the one at which you regularly bowl your league games; it should meet a number of qualifications I would like to submit for consideration before you choose your practice lane.

You need an atmosphere that is as quiet as possible. Therefore, find a lane and a time (or times) when you can be absolutely alone on the lanes. This may take some doing—even some rearrangement of your own schedule to fit the "dead" time at the lanes. When the bowling season starts in earnest in the fall, go to various lanes in your neighborhood or near your business and ask to see the schedules of the forthcoming leagues. You will always be able to find an interval either before regular league play or after a league has finished bowling when the lanes will have less play and therefore be quieter for your practice.

Ask the lane manager to put you on a lane away from other bowlers and ask him to keep other bowlers off adjacent lanes as long as possible. Make a friend of the lane manager. Ask his bowling advice about the conditioning of the lanes. Come to him with your problems. He'll usually be glad to help you, and as you improve your bowling skills he will take a great deal of satisfaction out of helping you.

Make the lane operator your friend and confidant. In many cases lane operators, especially countermen, are good bowlers and often good observers of bowlers. Tell the operator that your goal is to improve and that you would appreciate any help he or she can offer. This individual can do many things for you, such as seeing to it that you bowl against good bowling pins, that the lanes are surfaced well for you, and that you are left alone to practice. When other practice bowlers come in to roll a game or two, the operator can put them on lanes far away from you to insulate you from distracting noise and confusion.

I have used several practice methods successfully in my bowling career and I would like to recommend that you try one or all of them. They helped me raise my average from the low 160s to the 200 range within three years.

Perfect a straight-line approach to the foul line. Just as you put down a practice guideline in your own recreation room, a friendly lane operator may permit you to do the same thing in practice on one of the lanes. Use a Scotch type of opaque masking tape and put it down so that your approach straddles it. Use the masking tape as a guideline for several of your bowling lines. Set it up for a normal second-arrow straightaway shot and check to see that your feet do not cross the line. Using such a line will help you concentrate on squareness at the line because later, when you bowl without the masking tape, you will still see the taped line in your mind's eye imprinted indelibly on the lane. You can vary the placement of the practice delivery line so that you can work on an inside angle delivery, on a channel shot on the far right side, or on any angle you want to perfect.

Use two large sheets of paper with carbon paper between the sheets. (You will need the lane operator's consent for this practice.) Tape the sheets down beyond the foul line on the right-hand side where you normally deliver your strike ball. You will plan to make 10 successive deliveries, all supposedly strike balls, as if you were bowling the same ball to the pocket every time. After you have made the 10 deliveries, you will take up the sheets of paper. The carbon marks of the impact spots where the ball was set down on the lane will give you a great deal of information about the consistency or inconsistency of your delivery. If you see that you are varying by an inch or two to the right or left of your intended spot, you must work to make your footwork more repetitive, more exact. If the carbon marks show that you are lofting the ball out a few inches over the line in one delivery, and then a foot or more on another, it is an indication that you must perfect your footwork and timing so that you can reach the same proximity to the foul line each time you roll the ball. These carbon sheets can be prepared in sets and should be numbered and dated. If you use them frequently, you are bound to see an improvement in your bowling.

When you practice on any particular spare or split, be sure that you keep an accurate count of how many times you make the spare or split. I have found an excellent method of practice to work on the 3-10 right-hand baby split with my first ball of a practice frame. I aim for the 6 pin one time, for the right side of the 3 pin another time, and then try to chop the 10 pin off all alone. On my second ball, I have any number of possibilities for spare practice. I can practice on the 1-3 pocket, the 1-2 pocket, or even move Far Right and work on Far Left spaces.

If you hope to become a good bowler you must practice regularly both on the lanes and away from the lanes in the privacy of your home or office. The top professional bowlers practice every day, rolling from 25 to 100 lines trying to perfect their deliveries. I know that the average bowler cannot practice that much because it would be too costly in money and time. I do recommend that the average bowler try to practice at least three lines, or games, of bowling per week. When you practice bowling, do it with definite objectives in mind.

The first bowling in practice should be rolling the ball down the lane without any pins set up. This is called *shadow bowling*. Ask the lane manager to keep the pins up in their rack until you are ready to roll against them. He may even offer you a bargain price for shadow bowling since his pins are obviously getting less wear and tear than they would in a real game.

PRACTICE A REPEATING DELIVERY

Once you are ready to shadow bowl, really concentrate on achieving a machinelike repetition of your delivery. You want every delivery to be exactly the same as the one before, in ball speed, in tempo of footwork to the line, and in timing at the line so the hand can "squeeze" the ball properly as it passes the sliding left foot.

Since you will be practicing your strike ball you will want to emphasize staying down at the line as you deliver it, keeping your head down and your eye on your target spot at the darts, until you have watched the ball travel over your chosen spot.

Keep track of your deliveries. Use a notebook and enter your own analysis of each ball rolled. For example, you might note "five rolls, three over target, two inside," or "head came up too soon, pulled left."

Work on a consistent hand position at delivery, noting whether you are releasing the ball at the same point of your approach each time and whether you are in control of the ball (and not vice versa) delivering it out over the foul line 12 to 14 inches with "action" imparted by the fingers.

Work on your timing. Try to roll the ball at exactly the same speed every time. Perfect a consistent routine from the moment you step up to get your ball off the ball return until you have delivered the ball out over the foul line.

Picture yourself on television and imagine that the cameras are on you. See yourself going to the rack in good time, not too fast, not too deliberately, and picking up your ball, cradling it in the crook of your left arm. See yourself getting set on the approach, looking down to make sure your target foot is on the proper "dot" of the approach, then sighting your arrow or target line. See yourself taking a deep breath and exhaling before you begin your approach. Always remember to do that as the last act you perform before you start your pushaway.

In your mind's eye see yourself making a smooth delivery with a good follow-through. See yourself poised at the line in perfect balance having delivered a perfect strike ball.

I recommend that you use a stopwatch or a watch with a sweep second hand to time your delivery from the moment you step into the approach to get your ball from the rack until you have delivered it out over the line. Try to make this routine exactly the same every time, down to the split second. If you do you will find that you have standardized your delivery. Your confidence will grow as you know you have yourself and your bowling swing completely under control. You will become a better bowler if you perform the same routine every time you bowl.

SPECIAL PIN SETUPS

Once you have finished shadow bowling, ask the manager to set up the pins for you. You are going to work on making spares now.

With all the pins set up you will not attempt to roll a strike ball on your first delivery. On the contrary, you want to bowl two balls in every frame so as to get the most out of your bowling dollar. On your first ball, I suggest that you aim at the 3 and 10 pins, pretending that you are bowling against the 3-10 baby split. After you have rolled the ball note whether or not you would have made the split in actual play.

Having missed the headpin intentionally on your first ball you will have any one of a number of spare leaves to contend with on your second ball. You might try getting the 1-2-10 leave with your second ball. That means bowling into the 1-2 Brooklyn pocket and letting the 1 pin slide over to take out the 10 pin (remember it will have been knocked down on your first ball). You will be moving your target spot at the darts one board left so as to bring your ball into the 1-2 pocket.

As you make the 1-2-10 (imaginary 10, of course) you will also see that your ball will, no doubt, take out the 1-2-4-7. You have, in effect, practiced on two difficult spares at the same time.

Another variation of this practice spare bowling is to roll your first ball for the left-hander's baby split, the 2-7. It is a fairly easy space for a right-handed bowler because his ball is working to the left into the 7 pin and thus knocks it down more readily.

You will have interesting leaves after you knock the 2-7 down. Remember the principle of the target pin. Analyze each spare leave to determine which group it represents and bowl accordingly from the proper starting position, Far Left, Far Right, Strike Position, Left Center, or Right Center.

AWAY FROM THE LANES

Here are some tips on how to practice bowling at your leisure in your home or office. The first requisite is a vinyl-tile floor that you can polish to an approximation of the conditions you find on the bowling lane. Some dance wax will usually do the trick. Take some tape—adhesive or masking tape—and lay out a mock approach for yourself. Set up the foul line and a T-bar, the line on which you intend to practice. Walk the line many times a day, keeping your eye on an imaginary target over your mock foul line.

The idea is to instill in your mind the path you want to take on every delivery of the bowling ball. You can practice your first step, the distance, and the direction by putting a mark on the tape where you want your first step to be. Take your ball and, again watching your imaginary spot out over the line, make your first step and the coinciding pushaway of the ball. Then look down to see that your step has gone precisely the distance you want.

Practice intelligently and you are bound to improve. I am sure that you can and will develop practice techniques far more interesting and productive than mine. Good luck!

Judi has set up a mock approach in her recreation room. She uses a heavy iron to take the place of her bowling ball and practices her pushaway and her stride to the foul line, taking care to bend her knee as she slides and puts the iron "bowling ball" out over her imaginary foul line.

Practice making your first step of the bowling delivery in exactly the same way every time. With the mock lane in front of you, mark the taped line at the precise spot you want your first step to end. Assume a bowling position, start, and keeping your eye on an imaginary target down the line, step out without looking at your foot. Note how close you have come to repeating the step every time. Your first step is the most important. Work on it!

Equipment, Gadgets, Gizmos, and Gloves

Sometime in the 1950s a true innovation in bowling equipment and technique emerged—the bowler's glove. It had become evident that bowlers needed physical support to prevent their wrists from breaking downward from the overpowering weight of the ball when they first placed it into the forward swing. The earliest gloves had a pad that fit between the palm of the bowler's hand and the ball, acting as a cushion that kept the bowler's hand òn the side of the ball where he or she wanted it to be.

Later other experiments were made with the bowling glove. Now a great many top bowlers use a glove that gives them firmness, even rigidity, at the wrist. The fact that they continue to bowl with a glove is certainly an indication that the good bowler should consider using one, too. It may work for you as it does for the stars. Be careful to get a glove that fits your hand exactly. You do not want one with any play in it.

Recently another gadget has appeared on the bowling scene. It is a finger splint meant to position the right forefinger on the ball in the same place every time and prevent any downward break of the wrist. Another training device for bowlers on the market now that seems to have promise as a means to practice your delivery away from the lanes is a harness that fits your bowling arm and hand to keep you from letting go of the ball.

Any or all of the bowling gadgets or gloves may be useful to you. Try them all. They may improve your game.

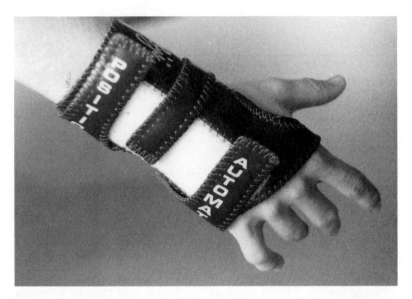

Many people have weak wrists and find it difficult to keep the wrist firm throughout the delivery. This wrist brace, one of the most popular and useful bowling accessories ever invented, helps the bowler to do so.

How to Keep Your Own Bowling Records

It is very important that you keep your own personal bowling records. All good bowlers keep track of their scores, splits, strikes, doubles, misses, and conversions of both splits and misses. By doing so, it is possible to gauge your improvement and notice both good and bad trends in your bowling.

Let me suggest a rudimentary system of record keeping that will be easy to adhere to and very profitable in the long run of your thriving bowling career. Get a three-ring binder and 50 or more filler sheets. A medium-size binder is best because you will be carrying it in your bowling bag. We all know that your bag is already as full as it can get holding your shoes, socks, bowling ball, and various medical supplies.

Here's the way you should set up your pages for easy record keeping:

Notes: "Arrived as first frame was starting, no warm-up. Hurried first game, one split, one miss, no doubles. Slowed down on second game and ball was moving better. Bowled second arrow until middle of second game when moved left one board. Kept second arrow until start of third game when moved one board left, same line, second arrow, and got string of four. Careless in ninth frame and no foundation."

Lane conditions: "Normal at start but running slightly at mid-second game. Must be alert for lane changes before I get nose-hits and splits. Must be aware of tiredness in third game and not slow ball. If anything, roll with more speed."

You should enter your statistics and keep a diary of your thoughts about your game as soon as you can after your bowling session has ended and your mind is still conscious of the physical and psychological conditions that affected your scoring ability. You can keep your book in a rough condition. Then, a day or so later, type your records or make a clean copy for neatness and emphasize the points you made in your diary. As you proceed from game to game, from one bowling lane to another, you will begin to build a body of knowledge about your bowling that will help you understand your own game better, thus helping you score better in the long run.

For instance, as you keep your records from week to week, it might become apparent that you are in the habit of rolling your worst game at the start of your series, in the middle, or at the end. If you notice a trend toward low scoring in the opening game, it might indicate that you are not warming up sufficiently before you start rolling. You will have to find some way to get more practice before you start. Many leagues allow only a shadow ball or two before the lights go on and the pin setters are put into operation. I have known bowlers who practiced tossing their bowling balls gently to each other from a distance of five or six feet as a substitute warm-up when they could not roll a line or two ahead of time. I will grant you that it is quite a trick to catch a bowling ball in midair, but it can be done if you are not afraid that you will drop it. Of course, you need a dexterous fellow bowler who will cooperate with you.

If you notice that you have a trend toward lower scoring in

your middle game, it might indicate that you are losing concentration or that you are not adjusting as quickly as you should to changing lane conditions. If you note that your last game is regularly your lowest game, it might be a sign that you are either tiring too soon physically or that you are not adjusting to changing lane conditions. If you know that fatigue is causing the problem, you will have to go to work on your physical condition to build up your strength and stamina.

The records you keep of your splits and split conversions will soon show a significant trend. For example, if you note that your wide-open splits are 5-7s and 8-10s, your ball is too weak and is not rolling into the 1-3 pocket strongly enough to get the 5 pin out.

When you keep track of your misses, you should also note which pin or pins remained standing after the miss. In that way you will note trends in your bowling that will indicate clearly where you need the most practice in the future.

Let's look again at the imaginary bowler's score sheet. Let's say that he has missed two 2-4-5-8 spares, and the numbers circled indicate the pins left standing. Once he left the 5 pin and once he left the 8 pin. It is obvious that his misses are inconsistent, with the ball rolling too far to the left and missing the 5 pin one time, then going too far to the right so that the ball never got back to the 8 pin. Several conclusions should be drawn: This bowler is rolling an inconsistent second ball. His trouble might be in varying his action on the ball at delivery point, or in varying his speed or line as he aims for this difficult spare. Leaving 2-4-5-8 spares frequently is a sign of a weak or inaccurate first ball. He is missing the spare both ways, with too weak a second ball or too strong a second ball. He must practice this spare until he makes it regularly with a strong ball that comes in from the right, hitting the 2 pin on its left side and then carrying on through the pin cluster to take out the 8-pin sleeper.

Your binder will be invaluable to you as you build several years or more of personal bowling records. You will find that as you progress up the ladder of excellence to true mastery of the game, you will be more and more conscious of lane conditions and the way they affect your scores, favorably or unfavorably.

Some lanes become known as high-scoring lanes and bowlers look forward to bowling on them. Others are known as tough, or "rock piles." These lanes are often excessively dirty and usually not as well prepared as the better lanes. Most bowlers dread bowling on difficult lanes because it seems that no matter how well you bowl, you never carry the strikes you feel you are entitled to carry and would carry under normal conditions. Bowlers come to know which pairs of lanes are difficult within bowling establishments. Many an unexplained absence in league bowling can be laid to the bowler's knowledge that he would have to face difficult conditions that night and wanted to dodge them.

The explanation for tough pairs is that sometimes there is a spot near the pocket that has harder wood than the rest of the boards; the board causes the ball to slide rather than act normally in its hooking action toward the pocket. The final action of the ball is different from what the bowler expects to happen. He might miss the headpin entirely or leave a one-pin spare under circumstances that usually would have brought him a strike.

With your notebook you will be able to anticipate problems with difficult pairs and look forward to the so-called easy pairs. Since psychological preparation accounts for from 75 percent to 90 percent of bowling success, you will be the master of your bowling fate when you hit a tough pair of lanes. You will have noted that in order to hit lane number 12, it was necessary in your last encounter with the pair to move several boards to the right on your approach and roll a faster ball to hit high on the headpin, thus counteracting the high board, or slippery spot, in the lane in front of the pocket. Perhaps you will not score as well on the difficult pair as you do on other pairs in the house, but you will pick up a few more spares and strikes than would another unprepared bowler who fishes for a game or two before finally finding the line and correction that were called for all along.

Here is another fact you must be aware of: bowling lanes are resurfaced at regular intervals. They are sanded until they are as close to being absolutely flat as possible according to American Bowling Congress standards—forty thousandths of an inch from channel to channel. The result is that your carefully assembled information about the way the lanes behave in a particular bowling establishment may suddenly be out of date and invalid. Not until the resurfaced lanes have been used for a while will they again exhibit individual characteristics, but if you are patient and continue to use your notebook, you will finally win out over the lanes. It is well worth the effort to keep your record book. It will give you an edge over the players who don't study the lanes so methodically.

There are several other reasons for keeping your own bowling records. Human beings and machines make arithmetic mistakes. You want to get credit for each and every pin you knock down. You can and should check your pin totals every few weeks with your league secretary to make sure your records and the league's agree. If you can keep your bowling sheets, by all means do so until you know your scores have been entered and totaled correctly. The sheets themselves are the best evidence. Once you know your scores have been recorded properly, you can throw them away or keep them as you wish. Many bowlers keep their best score sheets as a psychological reminder of how well they have bowled in the past and as an incentive for bowling better in the future.

How to Adjust to Various Lane Conditions

Many different lane conditions affect the way your ball reacts on the surface. Some of the surface materials add resistance to the ball so that it curves a great deal. Other materials such as oil cause the ball to slide and lose traction.

Basically, there are three types of lane conditions; the so-called normal lanes, the running or hooking lanes, and the stiff or nonrunning lanes. Of course, there are hundreds of variations in between these general designations.

The normal lane is one that causes your ball to react the way it does 75 to 90 percent of the time. Let us say that you are accustomed to rolling a ball at medium speed over the second arrow and seeing it move one foot left at the end of the ball track into the 1-3 pocket. For you, a lane that lets your ball react that way is a normal lane.

The running or hooking lanes cause your ball to hook too much. Your ball comes high on the headpin instead of into the pocket. It may even cross over into the Brooklyn pocket, the 1-2. Running lanes are ones that have not been conditioned recently or have been used a great deal without proper cleaning and surface preparation.

The stiff or nonrunning lanes are those that do not allow your ball to hook much. They have recently been conditioned and often are wet with oil. The ball is unable to grip the surface in its usual manner and skids instead of driving into the pocket.

There are several ways to adjust to various lane conditions, some more easy to effect than others. The most common way to adjust is to change your approach position, keeping the same target or line at the break of the boards. If the lane is running, your first adjustment would be to move your starting position one board left of your normal spot. The reverse procedure would be carried out if you found the lanes stiff: one board to the right at the start, keeping the same target line. Your adjustment may and often will be greater than one board to the right or left, but you should make changes gradually to avoid becoming hopelessly confused. Always note exactly where you are placing your aiming foot and which line you are hitting as you roll the ball.

You can also make target changes to correct your aim at the pocket. For hooking lanes, you will move your target at the darts to the right, or the outside. Move it to the left or inside for stiff lanes.

You might adjust the distance your ball travels on the lane by setting it down farther out on the lanes or closer to the foul line. Obviously, the farther the ball travels on the lane, the more the lane friction works to help it hook at the end. On a hooking lane the ball must skid farther; on a stiff lane it must skid less.

The speed of your ball affects the length of time the ball has to react to the lane conditions. More speed reduces the hook; less speed increases it. However, speed adjustment is one of the most difficult for any bowler to make. It requires a change in the rhythm of the footwork, and the result is often that the bowler reaches the lane either too soon or too late for a suitably effective delivery.

If you hold the ball higher in your stance, you can increase its speed; lower it, and you will reduce its speed. You can use a higher backswing to increase it. But I warn you, it takes a great deal of practice to be able to increase or decrease ball speed without disturbing the general rhythm of delivery.

Another way to adjust to lane conditions is to use a bowling ball with a harder or softer surface than usual. A softer ball will grip the surface better than one with a hard surface, so when you encounter hooking lanes, use a harder ball. When you hit stiff lanes, use a softer ball.

The basic rule for adjustments to lane conditions is "follow the ball." If your ball is hooking too far left, move left. If it is not hooking enough, move right. Furthermore, don't wait to make adjustments. After you have checked to make sure you are rolling your normal ball, make the move at once so you don't lose precious time to score.

OILY LANE CONDITIONS

In these days of mechanization the lane surfaces are, most frequently, conditioned by a machine which lays down the necessary protective surface. It also applies a thin coat of oil which affects the way a ball reacts on the lane surface.

Oil is slippery, as we all know, and when your bowling ball rolls on the oiled surface it tends to skid. The result often is that the bowling ball, which would normally start to move into the 1-3 pocket as it finally enters the last 20 feet of dry lane surface (that last important move into the strike pocket), is delayed a fraction of a second, perhaps even more than that.

When your ball starts missing the headpin on the right side, not "coming up," you can suspect that the oil applied to the front part of the lane has carried farther down the lane and is causing your ball to skid longer than usual and come up late or not at all. You can observe an oily track on your ball, too, which will confirm that abnormal condition.

Extremely oily lanes are the bane of every bowler's life. It is most frustrating, even for the seasoned professional, to challenge and conquer oily lanes successfully. Knowing that even the best of bowlers have trouble, you should accept the fact that you will, too.

The best way to solve oily lanes is to let your ball roll a little longer before it reaches the pocket. That means putting the ball down on the lane closer to the foul line than usual, not lofting it out onto the lane as far as you usually do. But that may cause your ball to "roll out," that is, expend its energy before it reaches the pocket and thus lose power at the pocket, deflect, and not cause a strike. You might even draw a split, sure proof that your ball has "died" at the pocket.

Another answer to extremely oily conditions is to forget about trying to get into the 1-3 pocket with your usual hook at the end. Move out toward the corner and try to roll as strong a straight ball as you possibly can. Your ball will need more speed and the hit should be high on the headpin. The extreme outside angle to the pocket should bring better strike action.

Be prepared to accept tough bowling conditions. Golf games are played in the wind, cold, and rain. Bowlers must play in some adverse conditions, too. When you encounter that difficult lane condition, accept it for what it is, and do your best to overcome it. Settle for making as many spares as possible. Stay away from the "nose" hit, high on the headpin, which causes so many splits.

See if you can't come out with a respectable score in spite of the difficult lane conditions. You will achieve a great deal of self-satisfaction, and your confidence will be built knowing that if you can bowl well on hard lanes you will be a much better scorer on favorable lanes, which are bound to appear in your future.

Understanding the Mechanics of the Slide

Bowling shoes are constructed in an unusual way. The right shoe is different from the left for the right-handed bowler. The sliding shoe needs to have a brake on the sole to keep the bowler from sliding over the foul line. The left shoe is usually made with a softer, chamoislike sole so that the left foot can slide easily. (The reverse is true, of course, for the left-handed bowler.)

As long as the bowler keeps his left heel up in the air as he slides to the line he has no braking effect. But the moment his left heel, made of soft rubber, comes down on the lane surface, the bowler's slide comes to a stop.

That is why the left knee must remain bent as the bowler goes into his slide to the foul line. At the last moment the weight of his body comes forward, straightens the left knee, and puts the heel brake down on the approach.

The last few feet of slide to the line are most important in keeping the bowler's body in balance. If the heel comes down too soon as a result of straightening the knee prematurely the bowler will usually pull his delivery to the left and roll an ineffective ball.

I recommend that every bowler make a practice slide with his left foot before starting his delivery routine. By doing so he rehearses in his mind the necessity for a smooth slide toward the foul line. Also, he carries out a check to see that he has not picked up any water or other foreign substance on the sole of his left shoe—material that might cause a premature, awkward stop at the line.

How to Control Your Speed

We are all accustomed to maintaining a certain set routine of rhythm in the delivery and the necessary arm speed which matches our footwork so as to get to the line at the proper time. Sometimes it is necessary for you to change your ball speed, speed it up in order to stop it from breaking too soon or slow it down in order to allow it more time to break.

Ball speed is one of the most difficult factors for every bowler, amateur or professional, to control. Remember that the faster the ball is rolled the more it will deflect as it strikes the headpin and bounces to the right. Imagine a car skidding on icy pavement: the faster it goes the less traction or "bite" it has on the road surface.

The slower a ball is rolled, the more bite and hook it will have. This statement is generally true but, on the other hand, when it is rolling more slowly the ball may exhaust its power sooner by the time it reaches the pocket.

There are three different ways to change speed. The easiest and most popular way is to change the height of your pushaway. By starting your pushaway from a higher position your backswing will also be higher and your ball speed will be increased. You will need to walk to the line a little slower to compensate for the increased time to complete your backswing.

The second way to change ball speed is to adjust the length of your approach. The closer you stand to the foul line the slower your ball speed will be with all other factors remaining the same. The farther back you stand, the more speed you will get. Try a few inches and not more than a foot for this adjustment.

The third way to increase ball speed is to "muscle" the ball, that is, consciously exert more physical power at the point of release. You will find this hard to accomplish and carry out smoothly. Furthermore, when the bowler muscles the ball he may not impart the same finger and wrist action that he does when he delivers his normal not-speeded-up ball. The ball may lose carrying power as a result.

There is another factor which must be taken into consideration when you attempt to speed up your ball. Putting the ball down on the lane an inch beyond the foul line and lofting the ball 12 to 14 inches out onto the lane are two entirely different matters. The first ball may begin to hook before it gets to the pocket, while the second ball may hook too late and miss the pocket.

Speed control is one of the most difficult phases of bowling to master. You will achieve it only through hours and hours of practice. But once you have speed control you will find your confidence is greatly increased. You can bowl well on any kind of lane surface.

Left-Handed Bowling

Most left-handed bowlers start out trying to learn the proper techniques of the game by mirroring the instructions for the right-handed bowler. For most of the fundamentals of the game this works very well, but there are many substantial differences between bowling right-handed and bowling left-handed.

It is most important for the left-hander to understand that he is bowling on a lane surface used only by approximately 5 percent of the bowlers. He has what is known as a "virgin track," one that has not seen a great deal of wear from the other 95 percent (of right-handed bowlers).

There are advantages and disadvantages to having a virgin track. The first detriment is that sometimes the track for the right-hander amounts to a slot, which almost automatically brings the right-hander's ball into the pocket. The left-hander does not have such a slot because, with less bowling on that side of the lane, a left-hand slot is never worn into the lane surface.

On the other hand, the left-hander has a much better angle

into his strike pocket, the 1-2 for him, by rolling his ball over the first arrow from the left. By rolling over the first arrow in contrast to the right-hander who usually rolls over the second arrow from the right, the left-hander's ball will deflect less as it hits the pocket.

Remember that the 5 pin is the target pin for either the right-handed or left-handed bowler, and the more directly the ball can get to the 5 pin the better the bowler's chance for a strike. The left-hander's ball comes in from farther outside on the lane—heads more directly for the 5 pin. Even if it does deflect to the left as a result of lack of ball speed or lack of finger action the ball may still get to the 5 pin and take it out.

While the left-hander will bowl from a greater outside angle than will the right-hander, it is most desirable that every left-hander learn to play all the angles just as the right-hander must learn them. Staying on the left corner or far left may not always be the best angle for a left-hander. When the left-hander learns to roll from all angles successfully he is prepared to bowl on any lane conditions he may encounter. He becomes the complete bowler without any weaknesses.

The left-handed bowler must be more careful than the right-handed bowler about pointing the ball toward the pocket. This may be a result of the left-hander's unconscious realization as he reaches the foul line that he is fairly well out to the left, perhaps too far, and must compensate for what he feels may be an error by pulling the ball or, as the expression goes, "pointing the ball" toward the pocket.

The left-hander must be careful to keep his bowling elbow in close to his hip so that he can make a straight armswing without any tendency to pull to the right.

The left-hander rolls the ball the same way every time from the same angle on the lane. Thus, he seems to learn his own game more quickly than right-handed bowlers learn theirs.

Some final advice for left-handed bowlers. Remember that you have a big advantage because you do not have to make major adjustments in your line the way right-handers do. Normally you need not play a lane any deeper or more inside than the second arrow. When the lanes are unusually dry, that

is, without oil or without much oil, the left-hander will necessarily move his starting position farther inside and roll the
ball out in order to hit the strike pocket. Remember, regard-
less of the lane conditions, to always roll the ball through the
target area. With proper adjustment for speed you will be just
as effective a strike shooter as the right-hander.

Don't Hurt Yourself Bowling

In the customary carryall bag, the bowling ball, bag, and shoes weigh more than 20 pounds. That is a lot of weight to be manhandled by the average bowler. You must be extra careful not to strain an arm or back muscle when you lift your bowling equipment at any time, particularly when you are taking it out of the trunk of your automobile. Always lift with your knees bent and your back straight, and you'll avoid a muscle tear. Use both hands rather than one on the handle of your bag.

I highly recommend the use of the bowling ball and equipment storage lockers which nearly all bowling lanes offer these days for a nominal price. If you keep your ball in one of the lockers it will always be at room temperature, ready for use. A cold ball just taken out of an automobile trunk frequently will cause moisture to condense on its surface, an unpleasant and unnecessary occurrence that adds another roadblock to good scoring.

Your bowling ball must leave your fingers at one last point as you deliver it out over the line. You will develop a callus or wear spot on one or more of your fingers from the constant friction between the ball and your fingers. If your bowling ball fits you well your chances of blistering are remote. But the beginning bowler who must struggle for a while to find the ball that fits him best will often raise a blister on one of his fingers.

Blisters are painful, as we all know, and it is important that they be treated in a serious fashion to get them to heal. They are distracting, too, and may cause the bowler to alter his delivery style to favor the sore finger.

To prevent blisters from occurring in the first place, the best strategy is to pad the potential blister area using a bowler's repair kit. Such a kit consists of a preparation called collodion that you can buy from your neighborhood druggist. It's a clear liquid that hardens to a firm but pliable surface after being exposed about a minute to the air. The bowler takes a small piece of cotton batting, moistens it with the collodion, and then forms it into a pad at the required spot. You can hasten the hardening by lighting a match and carefully letting the heat help to dry it naturally. After the first application hardens, you should put a second reinforcing pad on top of the first. You will also find a fine mesh cloth in bowling equipment stores. The cloth is a little easier to cut to shape than the cotton. Try them both and become an expert Doctor of Bowling for your own fingers.

There is a true art to such a repair. I cannot emphasize how important it is that you learn to put on one of those protective patches because—take my word for it—you will need help with your fingers sometime in the future when you are bowling.

I also want to warn you about the possibility of hurting yourself by unwittingly stepping in water or any other type of liquid that will cause your sliding foot to stick on the lanes.

Many years ago I bowled in a league that had a back entrance door. Bowlers would come from the parking lot behind the lanes and walk up alongside lane number one. When it was raining or snowing, of course, they tracked the moisture in on their street shoes.

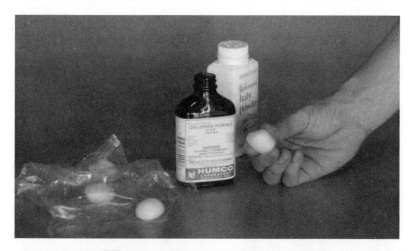

A bowler's repair kit—collodion and cotton—is used to protect an injured or blistered finger from the constant wear of releasing the ball from the thumb or any other finger. The box of baby powder is for careful use on sticky lanes. Bowlers have recently found that cigarette ash also works well on the sole of the sliding foot to increase slipperiness. It, too, must be used very carefully in order to avoid a foul.

In some way without realizing it, I got some water on the sole of my left shoe, my sliding foot. I went to bowl, stuck on the lane, tumbled head-first over the foul line, and seriously tore the tendon of my big toe. Years later, that injury still gives me occasional pain.

Every time you step up into the lane approach make it your universal habit to test the slide-ability of your left foot. Make a couple of short test slides to assure yourself you can proceed without sticking.

Learn to walk around the bowling lane with only your left heel touching the floor. In that way you won't pick up any unnoticed water on the carpet or in the restrooms. You may feel you look strange walking with your toe in the air, but if you do this it may save you from a nasty foot injury.

I would like to instruct you on the proper way to handle your bowling ball so as to avoid injury to your fingers or the

These two photos show the right and wrong way to pick up your ball from the return rack. Don't ever let your fingers get between the balls, or you may suffer a smashed finger when another ball comes back and causes a chain reaction down the line of balls. Always pick up your ball from the side with both hands on the sides of the ball and the weight evenly distributed.

muscles of your arm. Always pick up your ball with both hands at the same time, one on each side of the ball. If you should reach into the ball rack with your hands in line with the ball return, a ball coming back from the pit may come through at considerable speed and smash into your fingers, probably breaking one of them.

Do not pick up your ball from the ball rack by inserting your fingers into the finger holes. After you have gotten it with both hands, cradle it in your left hand until you are ready to begin your delivery.

Standing at the line with the ball still in your left hand, carefully insert your third and fourth fingers into the ball, locating them at the depth you want to use. Insert your thumb into the ball as the last act of gripping the ball. Then and only then are you ready to deliver the ball.

Bowling for Women

The Women's International Bowling Congress reports that there are approximately 170,000 leagues of women bowling in the United States at this time. It is also believed that there are another 24 million women who do not bowl in organized leagues but bowl occasionally with their husbands, families, or friends in so-called "open bowling."

All the foregoing instructions in the art and science of bowling for men are equally applicable for women with a single important exception. While I recommend that men use a 16-pound ball, the heaviest possible under the rules, I recommend that women use a lighter ball.

We all know, and accept as a fact of nature, that some women are not as physically strong as men. They can compensate for their lack of strength by learning to bowl with accuracy. These women can use bowling balls in the 12- to 14-pound range at first. Then, as they learn to control the lighter ball, they can experiment by adding weight to the ball in increments of one ounce at a time until the ideal maximum of weight and control is reached.

Obeying the laws of physics, the lighter ball will deflect more when it strikes the pins. That's an advantage when a woman attacks the 1-3-6-10 "clothesline" space, for instance. Her ball will bounce off the headpin and right down the line to clear up the spare handily. But the lighter ball has more difficulty getting into the heart of the pin setup to get that kingpin, the 5.

Because of the greater deflection and decreased carrying power of the lighter ball it is necessary for women to bowl more directly from the corner at the 1-3 pocket and at the 5 pin beyond the 1-3.

Women's wrists are sometimes not as strong as men's wrists. To combat that problem I recommend that women use a wrist strengthener which will help keep the wrist from breaking down in the backswing under the weight of the ball.

Many women, in my opinion, are too ladylike in their approach to the game. It is necessary for every bowler to roll the ball with respectable speed and authority. A woman should do everything she can to increase the speed of her delivery in order to counteract the loss of power and increased deflection in her lighter ball.

Remember that the speed of the bowling delivery is controlled by the height and actual "push" of the pushaway as well as by the speed of the bowler's footwork to the line. Moving back six inches to a foot or so on the approach will often give her the extra speed she needs.

Women must obey the same fundamentals of bowling that men do. Just remember, ladies, that you can be ladylike in your bowling and still deliver a bowling strike ball with speed and authority, imparting the squeeze that results in pin action knocking down all 10 pins.

Bowling for Seniors

Let's say you have never bowled in your life. At last comes that wonderful day when you are finally able to retire from work. No more early morning alarm clocks, lots of leisure time to do all the things in life you have always wanted to do.

Perhaps you head for a summer climate such as that of Florida or California. There you will join a senior community based upon your church affiliation or a new neighborhood you have chosen for the rest of your life.

Soon you will be aware that many retired people are getting a great deal of enjoyment from bowling with their newly found friends. Today, a great percentage of recreational bowling is done by the older retired person. There are magnificent bowling lanes being built at a rapid pace in or near all the retirement communities. They are clean, comfortable, and usually have attractive lunchrooms and bars. They even have "soundproof" childcare rooms to accommodate that grandchild who has come to visit.

You will find a great deal of friendship and comradeship if you take up bowling in your senior years. It's a lot of fun, especially if you don't take the game too seriously. You will make many new friends if you join a regular league in your neighborhood because the teams bowl against each other in round-robin fashion. You don't even need to have your own equipment if you don't want to spend the money. All leagues today offer rental bowling shoes and, at no cost, so-called "alley balls" with many different finger drillings.

If you take up the game of bowling in your golden years you may lengthen your lifespan because of your increased physical activity. Give bowling a try in your retirement. You'll be surprised at how much fun you'll have and how many new friends you will make.

Margaret and Bob Bolds, who retired to Palm Beach, Florida, about 10 years ago, find a great deal of pleasure and fellowship bowling in a senior citizens' league.

Faults

A very common fault is that of rushing the line. Instead of taking his time and delivering a smooth, rhythmic ball in time with his footwork, many a bowler will speed up his steps to the line. The ball does not have a chance to get back alongside the sliding foot at the line, resulting in a "dumped" ball, with no possibility of action being applied. The correction is for the bowler to make sure he paces his steps so that he arrives at the line not too early, not too late, but in perfect position to deliver an effective ball.

Another common fault is *slanting*. The bowler's second step goes to the left of his intended line, slanting in toward the center of the lane. If he realizes that he has moved into the center, he tries to move back out where he knows he should be and usually delivers the ball well to the right of his intended line. If he does not correct his slant he will roll the ball to the left of the pins. The correction, of course, is to straighten out the footwork so that it always takes the bowler in a straight line to his target.

One of the major faults the bowler must avoid is called side-wheeling and is caused by the bowler turning his body away from the necessary squareness to the line. The ball comes around the bowler's body and at the moment of delivery is thrown with the elbow out away from his side, causing an overturning action with the fingers on top of the ball and in no position to apply the squeeze. This fault will often cause a sore thumb.

This photo illustrates the fault of "topping" the ball at the delivery point. By allowing the fingers to pass the 3 o'clock position, the thumb is forced back beyond the 9 o'clock position. No action can be imparted to the ball, and it merely spins ineffectually off the thumb.

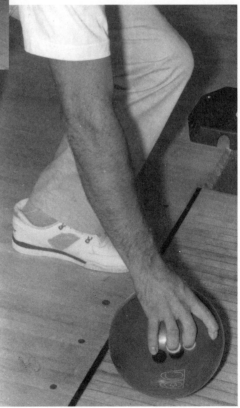

The bowler must avoid this common fault, the opposite of side-wheeling, caused by taking the ball back in a definite outside arc. The elbow gets away from its proper position close to the bowler's side, and in the downswing the ball is forced to roll on a line crossing to the left of the headpin. Frequently this type of fault will result in a topped action at the delivery point, with the fingers ahead of their proper position and in no way able to impart the necessary squeeze action.

A ball rolled with a backswing as long as that shown, high over the bowler's head, usually is delivered with excessive speed and rips through the pins so fast that there is not enough pin action to get a strike. Furthermore, the bowler finds it hard to control his direction with a long backswing. Correct this fault by limiting the backswing to no more than shoulder height. Roll a ball with good speed— but not excessive speed.

What to Do When You Are in Trouble

You must reconcile yourself to the fact that you will not always bowl well. If you can bowl well half the time, consider yourself lucky. Anyone can score well when he is bowling well. The trick is to score well, or at least not badly, when you are not bowling well.

Everyone, even the best of bowlers, runs into trouble occasionally in bowling. All of a sudden the ball that worked so well last week is flattening out or jumping into the headpin, leaving you nothing but splits or difficult spares. You start missing easy spares.

What should you do? Don't panic and begin to make radical changes in your starting position or target line. Consider whether the trouble lies in your delivery or in the lane conditions. Presume that the lane conditions are at fault, and make your first change by changing your angle as discussed earlier. At the same time, without changing your delivery other than the slight change in starting position, line, or spot, make sure you are throwing a live, active ball, one with action as a result of the proper application of the squeeze.

You may make a successful correction immediately and start scoring well at once. On the other hand, you may be in serious trouble, faced with problems on the lane and in your delivery. The corrections may not work right away, and you must realize that sometimes you will not be able to make the necessary corrections. You must reconcile yourself to having a bad night and make the best of it. If you cannot get strikes, try to get every spare. If you are splitting frequently, try missing the headpin on the right so that you cannot draw a split. Then get your spare.

As a last resort you might try a radical change. If you have been bowling a line close to the center of the lane, try moving out to the corner. Do something, even if it is only to relax your tension.

Keep a checklist of things you should ask yourself when you find yourself in trouble. I suggest that you photocopy this list and keep it in your wallet for reference when you need it. Read it carefully and understand what you should do. If you use it intelligently, it may save you from having a bad night. Always try to have a "good" bad night, one of those series when you escape with a respectable score when you know you really shouldn't have.

A TROUBLESHOOTING CHECKLIST

1. Is my wrist firm, with the thumb on the inside pointing to my usual thumb clock position, 10 o'clock or 11 o'clock? Is my grip secure, firm but relaxed?
2. I will check my starting position and my finishing position. Am I drifting to the right or left? Have I moved my starting position or my target down the lane without realizing it?
3. Am I rushing the line? Are my hips square to the line at delivery? Am I sliding straight at the line?
4. Am I rolling the ball at the same speed, or have I slowed it down or speeded it up?

5. Is my thumb getting out of the ball properly before my fingers? Am I giving it the squeeze? Are my fingers clenched after the ball is delivered, or am I opening my hand?
6. Am I actually seeing the ball go down my target line, or am I pulling out of the ball, cutting my follow-through short?
7. Do I have confidence in my ball, or am I aiming it into the headpin rather than letting it roll into the pocket?
8. Do I have a wandering elbow? Am I sidearming the ball or topping it?
9. Am I dropping the ball before I get it out over the foul line?
10. Am I lofting the ball too far out onto the lane?
11. Am I taking into consideration the fact that the lane conditions may be changing, may be running more than they were at the start? Should I change my line or my target?
12. I resolve to be more deliberate and take my time about each successive delivery.

Glossary

Action: The movement imparted to the ball by the fingers as the ball is released.

Alley: The playing surface of maple and pine boards.

All the way: Finishing a game with all strikes.

Anchorman: The last man to roll on the team.

Angle: The direction taken by the ball as it enters the 1-3 pocket for a righty, 1-2 pocket for a lefty.

Approach: The area behind the foul line.

Arrows: The aiming points imbedded in the lane.

Baby split: The 2-7 or 3-10 split leave.

Baby the ball: Delivering the ball without authority.

Baby split with company: The 2-7-8 or 3-9-10 split leave.

Backup: A ball that rolls or breaks to the right for a right-handed bowler, to the left for a left-handed bowler.

Balk: An incomplete approach in which the bowler does not deliver the ball but pulls up short of the foul line.

Ball track: The area of the lane where most balls roll.

Barmaid: A pin hidden behind another pin.

Bed: The alley bed, synonymous with a single lane.

Bedposts: The 7-10 split.

Beer frame: In team play, when all but one of the players score strikes, the one who doesn't must treat. Also any designated frame in which the bowler who scores the fewest pins must pick up a refreshment tab.

Belly the ball: Increasing the width of a hook from an inside starting angle.

Bench jockeying: Any type of conversation or other action intended to upset an opponent.

Bicycle: A hidden pin, same as barmaid.

Big ears: The 4-6-7-10 spare leave.

Big fill: Nine or ten pins on a spare or on a double strike.

Big four: The 4-6-7-10, same as big ears.

Blocked: A lane maintenance condition in which oil or some sort of lane finish is used to create a track.

Blow: A missed spare.

Blowout: Downing all the pins but one.

Board: A lane consists of individual strips of lumber called boards. Pros call them by number—5th board, 15th board, etc.—for targeting purposes.

Break: A lucky shot. Also a stopper after a number of consecutive strikes.

Break of the boards: The area on the lane where the maple and pine boards meet. Also known as the piano keys.

Bridge: The distance separating finger holes.

Brooklyn: Left of headpin for a right-handed bowler, right of headpin for a left-handed bowler.

Broom ball: A ball that hits the pocket in such a way that the pins scatter as though they were swept with a broom.

Bucket: The 2-4-5-8 spare leave for a righty; 3-5-6-9 for a lefty.

Channel: A depression to right and left of the lane to guide the ball to the pit should it leave the playing surface on the way down.

Cheesecakes: Lanes on which strikes come easily.

Cherry: Knocking down the front pin of a spare leave while a pin behind and/or to the left or right remains standing.

Chinaman: The third bowler in a team.

Chop: Same as cherry.

Clothesline: The 1-2-4-7 or 1-3-6-10 spare leave.

Count: The number of pins knocked down on first ball of each frame.

Cranker: A bowler who uses cranking motion to roll a wide hook ball.

Cross: Going to the left side for a righty. Same as Brooklyn. Going to the right side for a lefty.

Curve: A ball that breaks in a huge arc from right to left for a righty, from left to right for a lefty.

Dead apple, dead ball: An ineffective ball, usually one that fades or deflects badly when it hits the pins.

Deadwood: Pins knocked down but remaining on the lane or in the gutter. Such pins must be removed before continuing play.

Deflection: The movement of the ball from its true path caused by a pin or pins that are hit.

Die: Ball losing action or velocity at the end of a roll.

Dinner bucket, dinner pail: Same as bucket.

Division boards: Where the pine and maple meet on a lane.

Double: Two strikes in a row.

Double pinochle: The 4-6-7-10 split. Same as big ears, big four.

Double wood: Any two pins when one is directly behind the other: the 1-5, 2-8, and 3-9.

Dump: Dropping the ball at the foul line, usually as a result of rushing the line.

Dutch 200: A 200 game scored by alternating strikes and spares.

Error: A miss. Same as a blow.

Fast: In one section of the country, a lane that allows a ball to hook easily. In other areas, a lane that holds down the hook.

Fence posts: The 7-10 split.

Field goal: A ball rolled between two pins of a wide split.

Fill: Pins knocked down following a spare.

Fit split: Any split when it's possible for the ball to hit both pins (for example, the 4-5 split).

Flat ball: An ineffective ball with few revolutions, little action.

Foul: Touching or going beyond the foul line at delivery.

Foul line: The marking that determines the beginning of the lane.

Foundation: A strike in the ninth frame.

Foundation, early: A strike in the eighth frame.

Frame: One of the 10 divisions of a game, the corresponding box on a score sheet.

Frozen rope: A ball rolled with excessive speed almost straight into the pocket.

Full hit: A ball striking near the center of the headpin on a strike attempt or the middle of any pin you may be aiming at.

Full roller: A ball that rolls over its full circumference.

Getting the wood: Knocking down as many pins as you can on an impossible split.

Goalposts: The 7–10 split. Also called bedposts, or fence posts.

Graveyards: Low-scoring lanes. In a high-scoring center the term is applied to the lowest scoring pair of lanes.

Groove: The ball track in lane.

Gutter: Same as channel.

Gutter ball: A ball that goes into the gutter.

Hang a corner pin: Leaving a corner pin standing.

Hard way: Rolling 200 by alternating strikes and spares. Same as Dutch 200.

Headpin: The 1 pin.

Heavy: A ball that hits the 1 pin head-on or on the nose.

High board: A board in a lane that may expand or contract because of atmospheric conditions and change the track a bowling ball should take in that area. Most boards contract and leave a low area, but the situation is called a high board.

High hit: A ball contacting a pin near its center.

Holding alley: A lane that resists hook action of a ball.

Hole: The 1-3 pocket for a righty, 1-2 for a lefty. Another name for split.

Hook: A ball that breaks to the left for a righty or to the right for a lefty.

Hook alley: A lane on which the ball will hook easily.

House ball: A bowling ball provided by the center.

Inside: A starting point near the center of the lane as opposed to the outside, near the edge of the lane.

Jam: Forcing the ball high into the pocket.

Jersey side: The left side of the headpin for a righty, right side for a lefty.

Kickback: The vertical division boards between lanes at the pit end.

Kindling wood: Light pins.

Kingpin: The 5 pin in the heart of the pin rack.

Kitty: Money collected for misses. Used to defray expenses in tournaments or divided equally at end of season.

Kresge: While the 5-10 split is called the Woolworth, the 5-7 is often called the Kresge.

Lane: Playing surface. Same as alley.

Late 10: When the 10 pin hesitates and is the last to go down on a strike.

Leadoff man: The first man in a team lineup.

Lift: Giving the ball upward motion with the fingers at the point of release.

Light: Not full on the headpin, too much to the right or left.

Lily: The 5-7-10 split.

Line: The path a bowling ball takes. Also a single game of bowling.

Loafing: Not lifting or turning the ball properly with the result that the ball lags and lacks action.

Lofting: Pitching the ball well out on the lane rather than rolling it.

Looper: An extra wide hook ball, usually slow.

Loose hit: A light pocket which gives good pin action off the kickback.

Low: A light hit on the headpin, as opposed to a high hit.

Maples: Pins.

Mark: A strike or spare.

Match play: A tournament in which bowlers are pitted individually against each other.

Miss: An error or blow.

Mixer: A ball with action that causes the pins to bounce around.

Mother-in-law: The 7 pin.

Move in: Adjusting start nearer center on approach.

Move out: Adjusting start nearer corner position on approach.

Mule ears: The 7-10 split.

Murphy: A baby split: the 3-10 or 2-7.

Nose hit: A first ball full on the headpin.

Nothing ball: An ineffective ball.

One in the dark: The rear pin in the 1-5, 2-8, or 3-9 spare.

Open: A frame that doesn't produce a strike or spare. Also a miss, an error, a blow.

Out and in: A wide hook rolled from the center of the lane toward the gutter and hooks back to the pocket.

Outside: Playing lanes from near the edge.

Over: In professional bowling scoring a 200 average is used as par, so the number of pins above the 200 average is the number of pins over or in the black.

Over-turn: Applying too much spin to the ball and not enough finger lift.

Pack: Getting a full count of 10.

Part of the building: The remark referring to leaving the 7, 8, or 10 pin after what seems to be a perfect hit.

Pick: Knocking down only the front pin of a spare leave. Same as cherry or chop.

Pie alley: A lane that is easy to score on.

Pin action: The motion of struck pins that in turn knock over others.

Pin deck: The area at the end of the lane on which the pins are positioned.

Pit: The space at the end of a lane where ball and pins wind up.

Pitch: The angle at which holes in bowling balls are drilled.

Pocket: The 1-3 for a righty, 1-2 for a lefty.

Point: Aiming more directly at the pocket, high and tight.

Poison ivy: The 3-6-10.

Pot game: A competition in which two or more bowlers post stakes and high scorer or scorers win.

Powder puff: A slow ball that fails to carry the pins.

Powerhouse: A hard, strong strike ball driving all 10 pins into the pit.

Pumpkin: A bowling ball that hits without power.

Quick eight: A good pocket hit which leaves the 4-7 for a righty, 6-10 for a lefty.

Railroad: A wide-open split.

Reading the lanes: Analyzing the lanes to determine whether the lane hooks or holds, where the best place is to roll the ball for a high score.

Return: The track on which balls roll from pit to ball rack.

Reverse: A backup ball.

Revolutions: The turns or rotations a ball takes from the foul line to the pins.

Ringing 10 pin: 10 pin left standing after a powerful strike. Also ringing 4 pin.

Running lane: A lane on which the ball hooks easily.

Runway: The area behind foul line. Also known as platform approach.

Sandbagger: A bowler who keeps his average low purposely in order to receive a higher handicap than he deserves.

Schleifer: A thin-hit strike when pins seem to fall one by one.

Scratch: Rolling without benefit of handicap.

Set: The ball holding in the pocket.

Short pin: A pin rolling on the alley bed which just fails to reach and hit a standing pin.

Sidearming: Allowing the arm to draw away from its proper position during back and forward swing.

Sleeper: A pin hidden behind another pin.

Slick: A highly polished lane condition which tends to hold back hook.

Slot alley: A lane on which strikes are easy.

Snake eyes: The 7-10 split.

Soft alley: A lane on which strikes are easy.

Solid: A strong hit.

Sour apple: A weak ball, one that leaves the 5-7, 5-10, or 5-7-10 split.

Span: The distance between thumb and finger holes.

Spare: Knocking all pins down with two balls.

Spare leave: Pins standing after first ball is rolled.

Spiller: A light-hit strike in which the pins seem to take a longer time to fall than other type strikes.

Splasher: A strike where the pins go down quickly.

Splice: Where maple and pine boards join on the lane.

Split: A spare leave in which the headpin is down and the remaining combination of pins have an intermediate pin down immediately ahead of or between them.

Spot: The target on the lane at which the bowler aims. A dart, a dot, a dark board, or an arrow.

Steal: Getting more pins than you deserve on a strike hit.

Stiff alley: A lane that holds a hook ball back.

Strike: Getting all 10 pins down on the first ball.

Strike out: Finishing the game with strikes.

Strike split: The 8-10 on what looks like a good strike, the 7-9 for a lefty.

String: A number of continuous strikes.

Strong: A ball that has a good deal of action. Also working.

Sweeper: A wide-breaking hook that carries a strike as though the pins were pushed with a broom.

Swishing 7 pin: 7 pin left standing as other pins swish by it. Also swishing 10 pin.

Tandem: Two pins, one directly behind the other.

Tap: When a pin stands on an apparently perfect hit.

Thin hit: A pocket hit when the ball barely touches the headpin.

Tickler: 6 pin that bounces off the right kickback and knocks down the 10 pin.

Tomato: Same as pumpkin.

Topping the ball: When fingers are on top of the ball instead of behind or to the side at release.

Track: The path on a bowling ball that it rolls on most often; the path on a bowling lane over which many balls roll.

Triple: Three strikes in a row.

Tripped 4: When the 2 pin takes out the 4 pin by bouncing off the kickback.

Turkey: Three strikes in a row.

Turn: The hand and wrist action toward the pocket area at the point of ball release.

Under: In professional bowling scoring, a 200 average is used as par, so the number of pins below the 200 average is the number of pins the bowler is under or in the red.

Venting: Drilling an extra small hole to relieve suction in the thumbhole.

Wall shot: A strike that is aided by pins coming off the left kickback to knock over other pins.

Washout: The 1-2-10 or 1-2-4-10 leave. Also 1-3-7 and 1-3-6-7 leaves.

Weak 7 pin: A pin left standing after an unforceful hit. Also weak 4 pin.

Wire it: Throwing three strikes in the 10th frame.

Woolworth: The 5-10 split.

Working ball: A ball with action that mixes the pins on an off-pocket hit and has them scrambling with each other for a strike.

X: The symbol for a strike.

Yank the shot: Hanging onto the ball too long and pulling it across the body.

Zero in: Finding a consistent strike line on a lane.

Suggested Reading List

Anthony, Earl, and Dawson Taylor. *Winning Bowling*. Chicago: Contemporary Books, Inc., 1977.

Archibald, John J. *Bowling for Boys and Girls*. Chicago: Follett Publishing Co., 1963.

Audsley, Judy. *Bowling for Women*. New York: Cornerstone Library, 1964.

Aulby, Mike, and Dave Ferraro with Dan Herbst. *Bowling 200 +*. Chicago: Contemporary Books, Inc., 1989.

Carter, Don. *Bowling the Pro Way*. New York: Viking Press, 1975.

Day, Ned. *How to Bowl Better*. New York: Fawcett Publications, Inc., 1951.

Dolan, Edward F., Jr. *Complete Beginner's Guide to Bowling*. New York: Doubleday, 1974.

Kouras, Thomas. *Par Bowling*. Palatine, Illinois: Progressive Bowling Development, 1976.

Perzano, Chuck. *Guide to Better Bowling*. New York: Simon and Schuster, 1974.

Ritger, Dick, and Judy Soutar. *Bowlers' Guide*. Milwaukee, Wisconsin: American Bowling Congress, 1976.

Ritger, Dick, and George Allen. *Complete Guide to Bowling Spares*. Tempe, Arizona: Ritger Sports Company, 1979.

Russell, Don. *Bowling Now*. San Diego: A. S. Barnes and Co., 1980.

Salvino, Carmen, and Frederick C. Klein. *Fast Lanes*. Chicago: Bonus Books, 1988.

Taylor, Bill. *Fitting and Drilling a Bowling Ball*. Anaheim, California: Taylor Publishing Co., 1975.

Taylor, Dawson. *Mastering Bowling*. Chicago: Contemporary Books, Inc., 1980.

————. *The Secret of Bowling Strikes*. New York: H. S. Baines & Co., 1961.

Weber, Dick. *Champions' Guide to Bowling*. New York: Fleet Publishing Corp., 1964.

Weber, Dick, and Roland Alexander. *Weber on Bowling*. Englewood Cliffs, New Jersey: Prentice-Hall, 1981.

Wilman, Joe. *Better Bowling*. New York: A. S. Barnes and Co., 1953.

Index